CHURCHES
on Cape Cod

By

Marion Rawson Vuilleumier

Illustrations

Pierre Du Pont Vuilleumier

WM. S. SULLWOLD PUBLISHING
TAUNTON, MASSACHUSETTS

Copyright © 1974

by

Text Marion Vuilleumier
Illustrations Pierre Vuilleumier

ALL RIGHTS RESERVED

ISBN 0-888492-005-4
LCCCNI 74-80872

Printed in the United States of America

Contents

	Page
Introduction	7 & 8
BOURNE (North Side)	
Swift Memorial United Methodist Church	9
St. Theresa's Church (Catholic)	10
SANDWICH	
Corpus Christi Church (Catholic)	11
St. John's Episcopal Church	12
First Church of Christ (United Church of Christ)	13
Sandwich Friends Meeting	14
Forestdale Baptist Church	15
BARNSTABLE, (North Side)	
Chapel of our Lady of Hope (Catholic)	16
First Lutheran Church	17
West Parish Meeting House (United Church of Christ)	18
St. Mary's Church (Episcopal)	19
The Unitarian Church	20
YARMOUTH (North Side)	
Sacred Heart Church (Catholic)	21
Church of the New Jerusalem (Swedenborgian)	22
First Congregational Church of Yarmouth	23
DENNIS (North Side)	
Dennis Union Church (United Church of Christ)	24
East Dennis Community Church	25
BREWSTER	
Our Lady of the Cape (Catholic)	26
Trinity Evangelical Lutheran Church	27
First Church of Christ, Scientist, Brewster & Orleans	27
Brewster Baptist Church	28
First Parish Church, Unitarian-Universalist	29
Immaculate Conception Catholic Church	30
Unity	30
Presbyterian	30
ORLEANS	
The Chapel of the Community of Jesus	31
St. Joan of Arc Church (Catholic)	32
Church of the Holy Spirit (Episcopal)	33
Orleans United Methodist Church	34
Federated Church of Orleans (United Church of Christ)	35
EASTHAM	
First Universalist Parish of Eastham	36
Nauset Baptist Church	36
Eastham United Methodist Church	37

Grace Chapel (Assemblies of God)	38
Church of the Visitation (Catholic)	38

WELLFLEET
Chapel of St. James the Fisherman (Episcopal)	39
First Congregational Church (United Church of Christ)	40
Our Lady of Lourdes Church (Catholic)	41
Wellfleet Methodist Church	42

TRURO
First Congregational Church (United Church of Christ)	43
Sacred Heart Church (Catholic)	43
Christian Union Church	44
Our Lady of Perpetual Help Church (Catholic)	44

PROVINCETOWN
United Methodist Church	45
Church of St. Peter the Apostle (Catholic)	46
The Universalist Church of Provincetown	47
Church of St. Mary of the Harbor (Episcopal)	48

CHATHAM
Holy Redeemer Church (Catholic)	49
First Congregational Church (United Church of Christ)	50
First United Methodist Church	51
St. Christopher's Church (Episcopal)	52
First Church of Christ, Scientist	53
Our Lady of Grace (Catholic)	53
South Chatham Community Church	54
West Chatham Christadelphian Ecclesia	55

HARWICH
South Harwich United Methodist Church	55
United Methodist Church	56
Jehovah's Witnesses Kingdom Hall	56
Christ Church (Episcopal)	57
Pilgrim Congregational Church (United Church of Christ)	58
Holy Trinity Catholic Church	59
First Congregational Church (United Church of Christ)	60
First Baptist Church of West Harwich and Dennisport	61
First Church of Christ, Scientist	62

DENNIS (South Side)
Our Lady of Annunciation Church (Catholic)	62
Cape Cod Pentecostal Assembly	63
Reorganized Church of Jesus Christ	63
The Dennisport Church of the Nazarene	64
Congregational Church of South Dennis (United Church of Christ)	65
West Dennis Community Church (United Church of Christ)	66

YARMOUTH (South Side)

United Methodist Church	67
St. David's Episcopal Church	68
Bass River Community Baptist Church	69
South Yarmouth Friends Meeting	70
St. Pius The Tenth Catholic Church	71
Our Lady of the Highway (Catholic)	72
Baha'i World Faith	72
Evangelical Baptist Church	73
West Yarmouth Congregational Church (United Church of Christ)	74
New Testament Baptist Church	75

BARNSTABLE (South Side)

Jehovah's Witnesses Kingdom Hall	75
The Federated Church of Hyannis	76
Greek Orthodox Church of St. George	77
Cape Cod Synagogue	78
Faith Assembly of God	79
First Church of Christ, Scientist	80
First Baptist Church	81
St. Francis Xavier Church (Catholic)	82
Seventh-Day Adventist Church	83
Church of Christ	83
Zion Union Church	84
Calvary Baptist Church	85
St. Andrews-By-The-Sea (Episcopal)	86
Union Chapel	86
Craigville Tabernacle (United Church of Christ)	87
Our Lady of Victory (Catholic)	88
South Congregational Church (United Church of Christ)	89
St. Peter's Chapel (Episcopal)	90
Osterville Baptist Church	91
Our Lady of Assumption Church (Catholic)	92
United Methodist Church	93
Cotuit Federated Church	94
Saint Jude's Chapel (Catholic)	95

MASHPEE

First Pentecostal Church of Christ	95
Mashpee Baptist Church	96
Old Indian Church (Baptist)	97
Queen of all Saints Chapel (Catholic)	98

FALMOUTH

Waquoit Congregational Church (United Church of Christ)	99
Jehovah's Witnesses Kingdom Hall	100
St. Thomas' Chapel (Catholic)	100

St. Anthony's Church (Catholic)	101
Falmouth Baptist Church	102
St. Patrick's Church (Catholic)	103
John Wesley United Methodist Church	104
Saint Barnabas Memorial Church (Episcopal)	105
The First Congregational Church (United Church of Christ)	106
Church of the Messiah (Episcopal)	107
St. Joseph's Church (Catholic)	108
First Church of Christ, Scientist	109
Christ Lutheran Church	110
Unitarian Fellowship of Falmouth	111
United Methodist Church	111
West Falmouth Meeting of Friends	112
Immaculate Conception Church (Catholic)	112
North Falmouth Congregational Church (United Church of Christ)	113
East End Meetinghouse (United Church of Christ)	114
BOURNE (South Side)	
Cataumet United Methodist Church	115
Cataumet Christadelphian Ecclesia	116
Church of Jesus Christ of Latter Day Saints	117
First Baptist Church	118
St. John the Evangelist (Catholic)	119
Bourne United Methodist Church	120
St. Margaret's Church (Catholic)	121
St. Peter's Church of the Canal (Episcopal	122
Grace Alliance Church (Christian & Missionary Alliance)	123
First Church of Christ, Scientist	124
Otis Air Force Base Chapels	124
Addenda	125-128

Introduction

Imagine yourself looking down on the crooked arm-shaped peninsula of Cape Cod as it looked 350 years ago. It is blanketed by green forests, edged by golden sand and dotted with sparkling blue ponds. Here and there Indian trails crisscross the sunbaked land to points on either shore. Though occasionally a human voice is heard, it is the bird and animal sounds with an accompaniment of wind and wave that permeate this realm of nature.

The natives, who have lived here many thousands of years, are a religious people, worshipping the Great Spirit. Attuned to the world of nature and led by their magnificent spirited Chieftain Massasoit, they commune with the Great Heart Beat of the world, treading gently in His habitat.

The English, fleeing their religious oppressors, have barely arrived. Their ship, the Mayflower, has brought more than people. It has carried a worshipping community and a religious library to these shores. The faith of the Pilgrims and particularly the revelation of Jesus Christ has been shared with native friends as soon as John Elliot, Thomas Mayhew, and Richard Bourne learned the language.

So, in this long ago time, on this quiet verdant land, there a communities of worshipping people. In addition to the worship areas in central clearings and native shelters, there are meetinghouses sprinkled down the Cape. With every new settlement came the church as well as twon government. Sandwich, Barnstable, and Yarmouth were the first, with the West Barnstable congregation arriving as an established parish, having been gathered in 1616 in London, England.

The oldest building housing a worshipping people belongs to the natives, however, for with the help of Richard Bourne, the Wampanoags built a little Indian church at Briant's Neck by Santuit Pond in 1664.

At first the white men's churches were erected by Pilgrims or their spiritual descendants and were of the Congregational Way. But as time passed, the waves of great migrations brought others on pilgrimages from many nations. These first religious aliens were sometimes looked at askance by the "first comers."

Quakers came in 1654, causing some consternation in the towns, since up to this time church membership and citizenship were synonymous. Moderation prevailed, however, and Quakers settled down first in Sandwich and West Falmouth, then later in South Yarmouth.

Baptists caused the next wave, when the adherents of impetuous Roger Williams arrived. These people, joined by some from the established church, were the "Come Outers" referred to by Joseph C. Lincoln. Later the abolitionists who wished their churches to take a strong stand on slavery were termed this also.

The Methodist wave came crashing in force just before 1800. Itinerant preachers traveled across the dunes scattering small "classes" like surging foam. Cape Codders called them "New Lights."

Episcopalians weren't really accepted until after the two English Wars. They were "Late Comers," arriving after the Catholics who were whalers, fishermen, and factory workers at Sandwich.

After each wave, suspicion subsided and each differing congregation nestled into a favorable spot. A patchwork quilt of different but complementary congregations soon covered the Cape. More hues were added as others with still differing views arrived, including the many sect groups.

Now in current days, church life has burst into a many-faceted jewel. Since Vatican II the prismatic reflections are even more colorful and dazzling as communions of people dedicated to living God's will have made bridges toward one another as well as to God and outward to the world. The Cape Cod Council of Churches, the Craigville Conference Center, and other ecumenical endeavors bring a depth and tone to this religious scene.

One hundred and thirty-six Congregations now represent thirty denominations on Cape Cod. Some, like the Baha'i, have no buildings. Others consider themselves religious societies rather than churches. A few worship in non-church space or are planning for future buildings. A handful of chapels are summer only.

Space does not permit all to be pictured in this book, but each is mentioned in the text. A complete listing of all the religious bodies in the fifteen Cape towns can be found in the Addenda.

Congregations are usually localized by their buildings. Hence the arrangement in the body of the book as far as possible, is geographical. Know though that these graceful structures, with their steeples and towers pointing skyward, are only shells. The real church is the congregation, worshipping and witnessing to the love and power of the Creator of the Universe.

A congregation develops as it is led by its spiritual advisers. Hence the tremendous importance of clergy and lay leaders. An attempt to list all their names in this history, however, would preclude saying anything else! Thus they are not all mentioned, but they are hereby saluted!

It is to them and to the congregations that this book is dedicated, with the hope that their present and future witness may continue to be a vibrant, shining force that will influence for good the life in our Cape Cod communities and draw all of us closer to Him.

Swift Memorial United Methodist Church

WILLISTON AND PLYMOUTH ROADS, SAGAMORE

A primitive box-like chapel called the Meetinghouse at Scusset was the first house of worship in Sagamore (then called West Sandwich). When residents separated from the mother church in Sandwich, they built the old white building on the corner of Meetinghouse Lane and Old Plymouth Road. It was erected in 1838-30 and was large and commodious with gallery and choir loft.

On March 26, 1911, the present stone church was dedicated and given the name of Swift Memorial Church. This honored both Nathaniel Swift, who long ago had given the land, and Gustavus Swift of the meat packinghouse in Chicago, who had contributed almost half of the building cost of $25,000. Ordinary field stone was used in construction. These were brought to the site by horse-drawn wagon and by wheelbarrow -- a monumental task. The organ, the third in this building, was installed in 1971.

The present parish is alive spiritually to individual and community needs. Its church activities include The New Foundation for young marrieds, as well as groups for men, women, and youth. Community groups are also welcome here.

St. Theresa's Church (Catholic)

SANDWICH RD., SAGAMORE

The Keith Car Co. had recruited a number of Italian workers from Bologna, Italy. Recognizing the opportunity in America, they sent for families and friends and a large Italian colony developed. At first Catechism classes were held in town by the Sandwich priest. The first Mass was celebrated in the Masonic Hall in January 1912, though after that adults had to journey to Sandwich.

In 1918, Father George Maxwell began holding Mass every other Sunday using in turn Sempione, Kabyan, and Crennin Halls. He ministered heroically to the whole community during the ravaging flu epidemic of 1918.

In 1925, land was purchased from the Keith Car Co. for a church and Eben Keith, owner, contributed $500. Thomas Kelleher of Sandwich, builder of the Buzzards Bay and Sandwich churches, erected the church. It was named St. Theresa of the Child Jesus and was dedicated on June 6, 1926.

The church is an interesting example of picturesque Gothic usually associated with the English countryside. It retains a charming flavor of the traditional, though it has a shingled exterior. The ruggedness of the structure is emphasized by the interior exposed truss beams and the mellow, antique tone of the woodwork. This church remains a mission of Corpus Christi Church in Sandwich.

Corpus Christi Church (Catholic)

8 JARVES STREET, SANDWICH

Large numbers of Catholics came to Sandwich in 1825 from Cambridge and Boston to work in Deming Jarves' new glass making plant. A wooden chapel was built by them in 1830 on Jarves Street. Outgrowing this, in 1851 they built a large brick church called St. Peter's at Church and Willow Streets. The original chapel was moved and incorporated into the Sandwich Hardware Store.

St. Peter's Church was a handsome structure costing $25,000. It had a high spire surmounted by a ruby glass ball. The light reflected from this could be seen great distances and was a boon to mariners. A northeast gale in 1852 brought down the steeple and in 1898 the famous "Portland" gale caused cracks in the structure so, regretfully, the church was pulled down. Earlier, in 1865, St. Peter's Cemetery, the oldest Roman Catholic one on the Cape, was established.

The modern Corpus Christi Church was built in 1901, with dedication on July 7th of that year. Incorporated in it were bricks, stained-glass windows, and wood carvings from the earlier structure. In 1921, the Drew homestead near the church was purchased for a Rectory and the old Rectory was converted into a Social Hall.

The interior was again redone with natural wood and carvings by Alois Schmid in 1946. An old USO building was acquired later for a Parish Recreation Center. Though the church mothered several parishes, its only mission now is St. Theresa's Church in Sagamore.

St. John's Episcopal Church

MAIN STREET, SANDWICH

Episcopal churches (Anglican) were in the Boston area during the Revolutionary Period, but were not fully accepted in this country until after the War of 1812. The Sandwich historian, Frederick Freeman, became an Episcopal clergyman and conducted services in the village in the 1840's. The setting was the chapel in his private school, the Sandwich Collegiate Institute, which was located on Route 130 opposite the Dillingham House.

A Religious Society was organized in 1854, with 39 petitioners, one of whom was the son of the founder of the Boston and Sandwich Glass Co. Services were held in homes, then in Father Clinton Hall. In 1881, Rev. Hiram Carleton and his son bought the ancient Wing Farm, later destroyed by fire, and held services there. A church building was begun in 1889 on Tupper Road, but was not completed because of depressed conditions following the closing of the glass company.

The present building, with its weathered shingles, was built in 1899. The Parish Hall was built after the turn of the century. In 1963, another addition connected the two buildings and provided choir stalls, chapel, and modern kitchen facilities. The Rectory, located next to the church, was also purchased about this time. This functional church plant houses a beehive of activity as parishioners work at local and worldwide needs.

First Church of Christ in Sandwich

136 MAIN STREET, SANDWICH

In 1638 the oldest church founded on Cape Cod was gathered in the village, a year after "ten men of Saugus" were granted land for a settlement. In 1813, because of a theological controversy, the Calvinistic Congregational Church was organized, with the minister and the majority of the church members building a chapel on the site of the present church. The rest of the congregation remained in the building on the site of the present Yesteryear's Museum and in 1825 affiliated with the Unitarian Church.

Then in 1918 the Unitarian, Congregational, and Methodist Church (which had organized in the 1830's) federated. This continued till 1965 when it was voted to merge. The Methodist Church terminated its existence but the others merged to form the First Church of Christ in Sandwich with standing in both the United Church of Christ and the Unitarian-Universalist Association.

The present church building, erected in 1847, is a graceful structure. The steeple is somewhat like that of Saint Marylebone in London, which was designed by Sir Christopher Wren. Inside are such items of historic interest as an antique organ built in 1847 and noted for its "toothpick" pedal board, a 1715 pulpit Bible and a church bell cast in 1675. The parish is more than a custodian of history, however, for it has an active ministry to community and world.

Sandwich Friends Meeting

SPRING HILL ROAD, SANDWICH

The first Quakers arriving in Sandwich received a cool welcome. Church membership and voting privileges were synonymous in the first years of the Colony, where the religious pioneers were endeavouring to create a "Bible Commonwealth". Town officials puzzled over how to handle new residents who were not church members and did not wish to contribute to meetinghouse support. Nevertheless, seventeen families soon comprised the new congregation.

The Sandwich Monthly Meeting of Friends was established in 1654 and is the oldest continuous Quaker congregation in America. This meetinghouse is the third to be built on this site and was erected in 1810. The long sheds for horses and buggies and the peaceful woodland setting give an aura of long ago which is deepened as the visitor enters the simple structure.

The plain sanctuary on the first floor is divided in half so men and women could sit separately. When completely separate business meetings were held, the central wooden partitions were lowered from the ceiling. This was done with an amazing contrivance located in the upstairs kitchen. It resembles a ship's wheel and connects with the partition by ropes and two pulleys located in the attic. The second floor also has a large dining room. When Quakers came from all over southeastern Massachusetts for Quarterly Meeting, it was a two-day affair and meals were necessary.

Now the activity at the Meetinghouse is confined to regularly scheduled worship once a year on the first Sunday in August and to an occasional meeting for worship, business, or a wedding. It has two associated preparative meetings in South Yarmouth and West Falmouth. The cemetery beside the Meetinghouse is still used for burial of members and their relatives. Quarterly Meetings are now held in New Bedford. Friends continue to be active in their community and the wider world in their concern for their fellow men.

Forestdale Baptist Church

ROUTE 130, FORESTDALE

In the 1800's this church began as a Methodist Society, later becoming Congregational. Supply preachers then came from off Cape, traveling to Sandwich Depot where they were met by parishioners. Preaching fees were $2.00 a Sunday. After a time, supply preachers were secured from Mashpee. Perhaps because the Mashpee church was Baptist, the Forestdale church became part of that denomination also.

The building, a small frame structure, originally stood across the highway from its present location on land given by the Fish family. The surrounding cemetery prohibited any further addition. Therefore, when expansion became necessary, Mrs. Nellie Burke gave land across the street.

In 1953 the church was moved across the road. The sanctuary was enlarged and a basement added. This enabled the church to have classrooms, offices, and modern kitchen and dining room. In 1960 a Day Room was secured from Otis Air Force Base and moved next to the church. Men of the church finished the building into a modern parsonage, with extra classrooms on a lower level. The sanctuary has been recently redecorated.

A member of the Conservative Baptist Convention, the church reaches out to the community with missions as an emphasis. One of the organizations sponsored by the area churches is a Christian Athletes Association.

Chapel of our Lady of Hope (Catholic)

ROUTE 6A, WEST BARNSTABLE

This chapel of Spanish Monastic design is a reminder of the Portuguese fishermen who lived in the area when it was built in 1915. Rev. Father Downing, who had this church as a mission of St. Francis in Hyannis, had been educated in Paris and had done mission work in the Basque country. He determined to build a church resembling those he admired in the Basque area.

The fisherman theme was followed in the anchor motif which appears in the stained-glass windows and in the statue of Our Lady, situated to the right of the sanctuary. A statue of St. Jude has recently been added. A rounded stained-glass window over the main altar depicts Mary as "Rosa Mystica". Bricks were donated by the West Barnstable Brick Co.

Since 1959 the chapel and its surrounding area has been a mission of Our Lady of Victory in Centerville. Through the years it had only been open summers. In 1970, however, a heating system was added and the chapel has remained open year round. Nestled on a curve of old 6A, it is an unusual, but pleasing structure to see in the midst of early Cape Cod architecture.

First Lutheran Church

ROUTE 6A, WEST BARNSTABLE

On January 18, 1915, a small group of Finnish immigrants formally organized a congregation in West Barnstable with twenty-one charter members. Affiliating with the Suomi (Finnish Lutheran) Synod in 1918, the congregation carried on its entire program in the Finnish language from 1915 to 1943. The present church building was dedicated on January 22, 1924.

The English language was introduced into part of the program in 1943 and the congregation became a bilingual one. Increasing in membership, the church in 1956 had sufficient strength and resources to call its first full-time pastor. In 1962, the merger of the Lutheran churches to form the Lutheran Church in America was constituted and this church, in this new affiliation, began its new direction toward Cape-wide ministry.

The property to the rear of the church was purchased for parsonage use in 1965. Then, in 1968, a parish house addition was completed, containing Fellowship Hall, classrooms, and offices.

The church numbers among its members people of many ethnic origins from thirty-five different communities. Additional services are held summers in West Dennis and, most recently, in the South Yarmouth Town Hall.

West Parish Meeting House
(United Church of Christ)
MEETINGHOUSE WAY, WEST BARNSTABLE

Founded before the Pilgrims landed, the history of this church began in England in 1616. Dissenters from the Church of England met secretly, organizing the very first Congregational church. After continuous harrassment, the parish--with some 30 members and its second minister, Rev. John Lothrop--escaped on the ship Griffin to Scituate in 1634. Then the parish moved in 1639 to the great marshes of Barnstable on lands granted by the General Cout of Plymouth. The first meetinghouse was erected in 1646.

In 1717, after the east and west parishes were created, the present structure was begun, with the first service held here on Thanksgiving Day 1719. The golden cock atop the steeple is five feet across and was ordered from England. The Paul Revere half-ton bell was cast in 1806 and was a bequest of Col. James Otis, father of James Otis, "The Patriot" of Revolutionary fame. The church was the scene of Town meetings until 1849.

In 1852 the church was remodeled along neo-classical lines. Fortunately the church was too poor for a new building, so the shell of the original remained. In 1953, under the sponsorship of the West Parish Memorial Foundation, it was completely restored to its early grandeur. Its entrance is on the broad side and it has box pews, great oak timbers, and a high pulpit with sounding board. It is not a museum, however, for its sanctuary and nearby parish house houses an active parish. The parsonage is an ancient structure, but beautifully remodelled, where Chief Justice Lemuel Shaw of Massachusetts was born.

St. Mary's Church (Episcopal)

MAIN STREET (ROUTE 6A), BARNSTABLE

St. Mary's Church had its beginnings about 1880 when a group of summer visitors held services in the home of Admiral William Radford, just across the street from the present church. In 1882, services were held next door in the old colonial courthouse (then the Third Baptist Church). In the fall of 1888, St. Mary's Parish was incorporated and the first parish meeting was held. A gift of land was accepted and the cornerstone of the church laid in 1890.

At first the congregation was mostly of summer residents, though a handful of people kept the services going in winter. Officiating clergy came from Boston, but services were not held regularly until 1924 when a professor from Episcopal Theological Seminary was engaged. In 1928 the first rector was called and in 1939 the sanctuary was enlarged and a sacristy and study added. A parish hall was built in 1948, and added to in 1965.

The beautiful gardens surrounding the church were begun in the 1940's. Sculptures and plantings enhance the series of small gardens which in 1958 won the gold medal of the Massachusetts Horticultural Scoiety. Inside, there is a lovely old world feeling about the Lady Chapel, carvings, stained glass windows, the baptistry, and the creche. The parish endeavors to meet the needs of parishioners and the wider community. Prayer groups and healing services are held, in addition to Sunday services and Holy Communion.

The Unitarian Church

MAIN STREET (ROUTE 6A), BARNSTABLE

This parish was originally part of the first Congregational church in Barnstable which settled this village, having begun its history in 1616 in London. Led by Rev. John Lothrop, the parish escaped from harrassment in London and settled in Scituate briefly before coming to Barnstable in 1639. When the East and West Precincts were created, the East Parish church was built in 1717 on Cobb's Hill. The first building was replaced by another in 1836, which was destroyed by fire in 1905.

In the early 1800's when New England Congregationalism was split by theological controversy, this parish became Unitarian. In 1819 a minister of liberal tendencies was called, and it is assumed the church became Unitarian about 1825. It is now affiliated with the American Unitarian Association.

The present stately edifice was designed by Guy Lowell, the architect of the Boston Museum of Fine Arts. Art work in the church depicts religious symbols of all faiths, showing the all-inclusive unity of religious faith and fellowship. A parish house was added in 1960. The church also owns the Pilot House on Mill Way, the minister's residence, and the adjacent old school house. The latter has served as headquarters for the Cape Cod Conservatory of Music and Arts and now houses a used clothing depot for Church World Service, and Cape Cod Council of Churches.

Parish activities include the Women's Alliance and activities for all age groups. One of its major thrusts is in the field of social concerns.

Sacred Heart Church (Catholic)

SUMMER STREET, YARMOUTHPORT

The first masses in Yarmouthport began about the year 1878 and were held in a private residence. Then 25 years later services were moved to the Lyceum Hall.

In 1899, this beautiful country Gothic church, with its shingled exterior, was erected just off scenic Route 6A. It was a gift of Miss Jane Byrne, who was governess for the Simpkins family at "Sandy Side." There is a plaque inside in her memory. The designer was Elbridge Taylor, who also built the original Cummaquid Inn.

Though still much the same as when it was built, the church has been modernized to include electricity. A mission of St. Francis Xavier Church in Hyannis, its services are held year round. With the increasing population there is standing room only at most masses.

Roman Catholic Churches on the Cape began in three areas: Sandwich with the arrival of the Sandwich Glass Co. factory workers, Woods Hole with the advent of the whalers of Portugal and the Azores, and Provincetown when a large Irish Colony came from Boston and when Portugese fishermen arrived. From these three beachheads, over thirty churches were eventually established, one of which is this lovely brown church.

Church of the New Jerusalem (Swedenborgian)

ROUTE 6A, YARMOUTHPORT

In 1823 interest developed in Yarmouth in a new religious group referred to as the New Church. The full name was the Church of the New Jerusalem, taken from the Book of Revelation as interpreted by the Swedish scientist-theologian and philosopher Emmanuel Swedenborg. Hence the church is also referred to as Swedenborgian.

By 1843 a local congregation was formed by nine substantial citizens including Nathaniel Simpkins. Services were held first in Yarmouth Hall, then were held across the street in the second floor of what is now Parnassus Book Store. The church was one of the most influential in Yarmouth in the latter part of the nineteenth century.

The present building, across from the village green, was erected in 1870 and designed by an Italian architect. The church has one of the finest organs in the country. The congregation has always emphasized music and has established a tradition of "worship in the sphere of great music."

Services are held now only in the summer beginning in early July and extending to the Sunday before Labor Day. The building is also often used for musical recitals.

First Congregational Church of Yarmouth

MAIN STREET (ROUTE 6A), YARMOUTHPORT

This church was gathered in 1639, anteceding the incorporation of the town by several months. It was the seventh church in the colony. The original building was a log structure with a thatched roof located on Fort Hill near the Ancient Cemetery. In 1716 a larger building was erected in the lower end of town. Fifty years later it was enlarged. The third building was constructed in 1830 on the common--the present day Yarmouth Playground.

The fourth and present building was constructed in 1879, and in 1892 the pipe organ now in use was given by Dr. Azariah Eldridge. The steeple, a landmark for ships, was blown down and replaced twice, in 1947 and again in 1956.

A parsonage was purchased in 1966. In 1968 the 1850 Bray house was given to the church by the Perera family and was converted into the present Parish House.

This parish was the parent of the West Yarmouth Congregational Church and sponsored the Friday Club, a benevolent organization still in existence. The Women's Fellowship and the Meeteneets are among the organizations of the parish which reach out to community and world. It is a member of the National Association of Congregational Christian Churches.

Dennis Union Church
(United Church of Christ)

ROUTE 6A, DENNIS

Dennis was once called the East Precinct of Yarmouth, and residents traveled to that town to church. Then on February 28, 1721, six freeholders established a congregation in the home of Nathaniel Howes. In 1725-26 Josiah Dennis for whom the town was named, began his ministry and was later ordained here. An early church building, known as the Nobscusset Meetinghouse, was later rolled to several locations serving the town as a school, tin shop, slaughterhouse, and garage. Its timbers are now incorporated in the Cape Playhouse.

The original congregation split into several groups including the Unitarians who met in private homes, the Methodists who met in Carlton Hall, and the Evangelical Congregational Society which built the present building in 1828. In 1866 these groups came together as the Dennis Union Religious Society. In 1878 the Bell Circle, made up of young ladies of the town, bought a bell and a clock for the tower. Prior to that worshippers were called with the schoolhouse handbell.

A Parish House addition was built onto the church in 1954 with all bills paid on Dedication Day. Friends of Gertrude Lawrence contributed the stage and lighting in the Fellowship Hall in memory of the star. The Sanctuary was redecorated and the old gallery restored in 1969.

Since this is the only church in the village, there is a community ministry through its organizations and as it provides a meeting place for other groups.

East Dennis Community Church

CENTER STREET, EAST DENNIS

The old Red Top Cemetery in West Brewster was the site of the first home of this church. The congregation held meetings there beginning about 1820 in a small frame building on Stony Brook Road. It was called then the Wesleyan Methodist Society of East Dennis and Brewster.

The current site in East Dennis was purchased in 1845 and a wooden church erected. It was similar to the present structure, but had only a sanctuary and balcony room.

In 1927, the church had a legacy of $200,000 for a new church and parsonage of brick or stone. When the legacy became available, after the death of an heir, in 1945, there was much discussion of the exterior finish, since brick or stone would not fit the village architecture. In 1955, the problem was legally solved by planning a concrete, fireproof structure as a base with a white wooden clapboard exterior. A parsonage was purchased on nearby Pleasant Street.

The new church was finished in 1957, then the old church was torn down. The modern plant includes a Fellowship Hall, offices, parlor, and kitchen. Classrooms are being added in 1974.

The name was changed and it was officially incorporated in 1954. It is an independent church, governed by the Church Council. Its parish emphasizes Bible classes for all ages and has a continuous chain of prayer.

Our Lady of the Cape (Catholic)

STONY BROOK ROAD, WEST BREWSTER

This new parish was established in 1961 by the Fall River Diocese with ground breaking ceremonies December 8 of that year. Since it is in a resort area, the building was planned with a divider. There is seating for 200 in the heated, winter section. The church can accommodate 500 more by opening the summer section. The altar can be rotated with a turning mechanism, to suit summer and winter needs. The basement area of the church has an auditorium with stage, kitchen facilities, and classrooms for religious education.

The theme of the church decor is the sea. The fourteen large windows have Biblical sea scenes. The sanctuary lamps and candelabra form anchors. A fisherman's net is over the altar area. The baptismal font is shaped like a giant deep sea clam. The carpeting is yellow to resemble sand and the ceiling is blue for the sky.

The statue of Mary stands on a map of Cape Cod. Her feet were designed to rest on the three Cape towns which comprise the parish of the church.

A mission of this church is the Immaculate Conception Church in East Brewster.

Ecumenism is emphasized here with services of Christian Unity celebrated. Other activities include retreats, religious instruction for children, as well as adult lecture and discussion classes.

Trinity Evangelical Lutheran Church

BREWSTER

In 1947, Rev. Christian Moldstad retired to this town and felt the need for a Lutheran Church. He was at that time operating the old Captain Winslow Knowles house as a year-round Inn called "The Manse." Services were conducted in the circular sun parlor of this building. Called the Lutheran Chapel, it had lectern, hymnals, and seating for twenty-five. In the summer the congregation overflowed into the living room.

In 1970, services were held in the basement area of the Moldstad's newer small house. Now services and adult Bible classes are held in the Brewster Town Hall. Plans are under way for a building to be located at the corner of Route 6A and Lower Road. Goals are to grow in faith and membership, erect a building and continue aiding worldwide Lutheran missions.

First Church of Christ, Scientist, Brewster & Orleans

ROUTE 6A, BREWSTER

The first interest in Christian Science in the Brewster-Orleans area was reported in 1889. Then during the summers of 1891-92, five women met in Orleans to study Mary Baker Eddy's "Science and Health with Key to the Scriptures." Between 1904 and 1913 Sunday services were held in private homes. Wednesday evening testimonials began the summers of 1926-27. In 1928 the Sunday services were moved to the Orleans Town Hall, with Brewster and Eastham residents attending also.

On July 26, 1929, the Christian Science Society was formally organized as a branch of the Mother Church, the First Church of Christ, Scientist, in Boston. In the summer of 1934 the testimonial services were held in the Universalist Church of Orleans. The first Christian Science lecture was held that July. The name of the church was changed several times but finally became First Church of Christ, Scientist, Brewster and Orleans in 1942.

The land for the present church was given in 1940 by Miss Faith Bickford. The building, of simple, classic design, was dedicated in March of 1942.

A reading room is maintained in the Orleans business district. Free literature is distributed to various places of business, and a free lecture is sponsored yearly. Members also hold services and distribute literature in correctional institutions.

Brewster Baptist Church

(AMERICAN BAPTIST)
ROUTE 6A, BREWSTER

Before 1812 there were only 3 or 4 Baptists in town. Occasionally an itinerant Baptist minister would stop by and preach. Then Nathaniel Hopkins invited Rev. James Barnaby to hold meetings in his home and eventually about 50 people formed a Baptist church in West Harwich. (Brewster was at first part of Harwich.) The church was formally organized in 1824.

In 1828, a plain church structure was erected by the congregation on or near the site of the present house of worship. The church building now standing was built in 1860. Thirteen years later it was remodeled and a parsonage built. The tapering spire of the church was struck by lightning in 1881, causing another period of redecorating and remodeling. This replacement steeple was lower and wider, no doubt in the hope it would not attract lightning. A baptistry was added in 1888.

This steeple was found to be unstable in 1912 and it was rebuilt, with a front vestibule being added to the building. More space was needed, with increased population and members, so a Social Hall and new kitchen were constructed; and the old hall was made into classrooms in 1953.

In recent years there has been a tremendous increase in members and in home and foreign missions, White Cross sewing being only one of many areas of outreach. Sanctuary and classrooms are overflowing with people and a new building program is in the planning stages.

First Parish Church, Unitarian-Universalist

MAIN STREET (ROUTE 6A), BREWSTER

The above church was organized as a Congregational Church on October 16, 1700, when the town was then part of Harwich. The building, erected in 1834, is the third meetinghouse on this site. The early town cemetery is located around the church and graves of many church elders, Revolutionary soldiers, and famous sea captains may be identified. There were ninety-nine ship captains who called Brewster home.

Formerly known as the Church of the Captains, the church has pews which bear brass plates engraved with the names of many of the town's sea captains. There is also a display of early American flags, some of which were used before the Revolution. The Parish House is historic Dawes Hall.

Around the year 1864, the church became Unitarian. The celebrated Horatio Alger, Jr., a Unitarian, served as minister of this church from 1864 to 1866.

This parish and the First Parish Universalist Church of Eastham were merged in 1971 and are known as the First Unitarian-Universalist Society of Cape Cod. Sunday services are held in Eastham at the Chapel in the Pines the first Sunday of each month and in Brewster all other Sundays.

Immaculate Conception Catholic Church

ROUTE 6A, EAST BREWSTER

Built in 1906, this church has been a mission of several churches, including the St. Joan of Arc Church in Orleans. The wooden frame structure is of simple design with a large, square enclosed tower in the front. In 1931-32 the east wing was added. The west wing was built on in 1968.

For a brief time this church was a full parish, when Father Joseph Nolin of the LaSalette Fathers was sent here to build a new church. The Our Lady of the Cape parish was established in April of 1961 and in 1963 when the new church was dedicated, the newer structure in West Brewster became the headquarters. Thus the Immaculate Conception church resumed its mission status.

Open now for services only in summer, the church serves as activity center for both Brewster churches the rest of the year. It also houses the Women's Guild Thrift Shop during the off season months.

Unity

Although there are no officially established congregations on Cape Cod, Unity members meet regularly in homes on various parts of the Cape. These members are associated with Christ Church Unity in Brookline. Also, they are connected with Unity Headquarters in Lee Summit, Missouri.

Presbyterian

Although there is officially no Presbyterian Church on Cape Cod, several families are meeting together one evening a week to explore the possibility of establishing such a church. About two dozen people, who are affiliated elsewhere with the Presbyterians, form the nucleus of this fellowship. Meetings are held in the hall of the Cape Cod Conservatory of Music and Arts.

The Chapel of the Community of Jesus

ROCK HARBOR, ORLEANS

Viewed from Rock Harbor, the new chapel of the Community of Jesus (an abbey-like Christian community of some seventy-five men, women, and children) appears to be an extension of Bethany, the Community's beautiful, Dutch Colonial retreat house. With a seating capacity of 250, it is an answer to much prayer, their previous "chapel" being a converted pump house which held 28.

Ground was broken Easter morning, 1972, and construction proceeded as the Lord provided the funds. The men in the Community helped wherever they could, and the first service was held four months later, on Ascension Day, August 6, 1972, with the Community's priest in residence, celebrating the Eucharist. The public is welcome to Holy Communion on Sundays at 8:30 A.M., and an open teaching on Monday evenings at 8:00 P.M., by the Community's founders and directors, Cay Andersen and Judy Sorensen.

Like the organ, which came from a former Sandwich Church (now a doll museum) and is believed to be the oldest tracker organ on Cape Cod, the pews and bell were gifts. The former were rescued from a condemned chapel at Ft. Devens, the latter from a dismantled life-saving station. Other points of interest include the sweeping roof arches of Carolina hard pine that direct the eye to two vertical windows behind the altar which are topped by a peaked lintel window, giving the impression of a doorway to the sky. Suspended above the altar is a massive gold cross of welded anchor chain, symbolizing the lives of the Community members joined together in His service.

St. Joan of Arc Church (Catholic)

104 BRIDGE ROAD, ORLEANS

At the turn of the century, Catholics in Orleans were part of the parish of Woods Hole. Mass was offered every six weeks for the people at this end of the very large parish.

After the Fall River Diocese was established in 1904, the reorganization gave responsibility for the Orleans members to Harwich parish. In 1931, when Holy Trinity Church in West Harwich was established, priests from that church ministered to Orleans residents.

It was in 1947 that the present Joan of Arc Church was erected, along with a Rectory. The parish included the towns of Eastham, Brewster, and Dennis along with Orleans. In 1952 this church began the first Catholic school on Cape Cod, St. Joan of Arc Parish Parochial School. The Sisters of Divine Providence came from their Mother House in Pittsburgh to be the teachers. The school closed in 1969 because of the shortage of teaching sisters.

In 1969, the church was remodeled and a beautiful new carved altar added. Thus the chancel was made more fitting for the new liturgical services. In 1970, a new hall was added, which has given a new dimension to parish activities and provided one of the best functional buildings on the lower Cape.

Church of the Holy Spirit (Episcopal)

MONUMENT ROAD, ORLEANS

Although this church was organized in 1933 with seventeen members, ground was not broken for the church building until 1935. Land was given by the Richard Kimballs. He was a retired writer, who later became lay preacher and then minister of the church. Mrs. Kimball formed the Craft Guild of craftsmen and women, who supply the Galley West Shop which is open each summer.

The 50-seat church was inadequate almost from its opening day, so in 1938 the size of the church was doubled. Part of the original structure was from the wrecked clipper "Orissa," which gave an interesting nautical effect. Other old beams came from the Chequessett Inn in Wellfleet. A Sunday School building was also constructed, mostly with volunteer labor, which has been a feature of the church's development. Additions are still continuing, as the church ministers to parish and community needs. The effect is of a pleasant, welcoming, weather-beaten compound.

The late Cape artist Vernon Smith carved many of the beautiful appointments. Among these are the carved doors, the flames on the pulpit, and the cross above the altar. Alert to spiritual as well as other human needs, the church has Bible and inquirers' classes, as well as a daily published prayer list for the Diocese at home and mission stations overseas.

Orleans United Methodist Church

MAIN STREET, ORLEANS

At first Methodism was spread over the Cape by itinerant or circuit preachers and by Camp-meetings. In 1820 a Reformed Methodist Church was organized and a meeting-house built in Orleans on the corner of Main Street and Route 6A. This church was closed in 1830, and on September 6, 1836, a Methodist Episcopal Church was organized with sexteen members. The old building was torn down and the cornerstone of a new building was laid in 1838 in its present location. The church and society comprised about one-fifth of the inhabitants of the town.

About the turn of the century many improvements were made, including a new tower, bell, and memorial stained-glass windows. A choir and a library were begun also. Since 1922, the parish has been associated with several different other Methodist parishes. Now, it is joined with the Eastham United Methodist Church.

Extensive enlarging and remodeling began in 1954, just after the church was incorporated. The building was completed in March of 1956. A busy program is designed to serve parishioners and the wider community.

Federated Church of Orleans
(United Church of Christ)
MAIN STREET, EAST ORLEANS

The Congregational Society was organized by a small company of Pilgrims from the Plymouth Colony, who founded the Plantation of Nauset in 1644. The first meetinghouse was built in 1646 on the north side of Town Cove, in what is now Eastham. One of the early ministers was Rev. Samuel Treat, who served the Indians, too. He wrote sermons in the Indian tongue for his native helpers to preach. At one time there were 500 Praying Indians in four villages in his care along with English parishioners.

In 1718, the Society received a gift of land and a meeting-house was erected on the present site. In 1829, this edifice replaced the earlier one. In remodeling during 1889, the sanctuary was moved to the second floor and a vestry built beneath.

A group of members left in 1838 to form the Universalist Society. Their meetinghouse was built on Main Street also. In 1939, the Congregational and Universalist Societies reunited to form the Federated Church. The Universalist building is now the home and Museum of the Orleans Historical Society.

In recent years the increase of population and summer visitors called for more facilities. In 1968, an addition containing classrooms, offices, and parlor was built. The Federated Church also added an elevator to assist the elderly. The parish continues its mission outreach as well as community concern.

First Universalist Parish of Eastham

SAMOSET ROAD, EASTHAM

On August 12, 1889, twenty-three members organized the first Universalist Parish in Eastham. Services were held in the Town Hall. Captain Edward Penniman headed the subscription drive for a new church. On a site donated by W. H. Nickerson a "pretty" church 40 by 50 feet was built. Because many members donated labor, the cost was held to $2,300.

Also referred to as the Chapel in the Pines, the church is of wooden construction, set in a wooded grove. It is of Victorian Gothic design with interesting small steeple. By the time it was dedicated in January of 1890, membership had climbed to forty-nine and a Sunday School had been organized.

Between 1936 and 1951, the church was open only in summer. By 1951 it was reopened full time with a children's choir organized and a Sunday School revived. The Ladies Circle did much during these latter years to modernize the physical plant. The church emphasized a music ministry, which extended to the community when it furnished quarters for the Cape Cod Conservatory's extension school. According to the church booklet of 1958 "We look back with pleasure and forward with faith."

This church joined forces with the First Unitarian Parish of Brewster in 1963 to jointly hire a minister. In 1971, the two churches formally merged into the First Unitarian-Universalist Society of Cape Cod. Services are held here the first Sunday of each month and in Brewster all other Sundays.

Nauset Baptist Church

EASTHAM

About the year 1966 members of this church began meeting in homes in the area. Then services were held in the Eastham Town Hall. Now members hold worship services and Sunday School classes in the Orleans Town Office Building. Midweek prayer and Bible study meetings are held in homes.

In 1970, steps were taken to purchase four acres of land on Route 6 where, some time in the future, a church will be erected. A member of the Conservative Baptist Association, the church is increasing from small beginnings. Though now served by an interim minister, services of a full-time pastor are eventually contemplated.

Eastham United Methodist Church

ROUTE 6, EASTHAM

The first Methodist Camp Meeting on Cape Cod, held in Wellfleet on August 19, 1819, led to the formation of this church. A circuit preacher visited often, encouraging the faithful and a class was formed. In 1821, a meetinghouse was built and the "class paper" showed sixty members. The building, according to Enoch Pratt's History of Eastham, "is a neat and commodious house, sufficiently large to accommodate all who belong to the society and attend the meetings, being at the present time nearly two-thirds of all the inhabitants of the town." The site of this first church is unknown.

At first the parish was connected with Wellfleet, but in 1823 the petition of separation was granted. A large white church was built in 1851 on the site of the Evergreen Cemetery at a cost of $4,900. It was a landmark for ships at sea. This building burned in 1920 and for six years the Methodists were without a church building.

The present church was built in 1926, then in 1953 it was moved farther back and a basement added. The church was enlarged again in 1964, allowing for more classrooms and sanctuary space.

The Fisherman's Players, a church-sponsored drama program began here. It has since graduated to a home of its own and is backed by the Methodist Conference. This active parish is joined with that of Orleans United Methodist Church.

Grace Chapel (Assemblies of God)

EASTHAM

About the year 1952 an interdenominational Bible study group was formed, meeting in a home in South Wellfleet. Many members came from the military installation at Truro. Gradually the membership grew and the nucleus formed this church.

On September 13, 1970, it officially came into existence and began meeting Sundays in the Eastham Town Hall. Services include worship, church school, and an evening evangelistic meeting. Bible study continues in homes. The congregation also has Christ's Ambassadors for youth and the Women's Missionary Council.

Plans are under way for a church, with a building fund being currently raised and land purchase in view.

National headquarters are in Springfield, Missouri, and the District headquarters for Southern New England are in Auburn. Nearby Charlton is the site for the Campground which hosts many groups for conferences and meetings.

Church of the Visitation (Catholic)

MASSASOIT ROAD, NORTH EASTHAM

In 1952, this church was built as a mission of St. Joan of Arc Church in Orleans. It is a frame building, Cape Cod style, with open beam construction inside. Designed in cruciform style, the altar is in the center.

In 1970, a new altar was installed with a base of wrought iron and carvings done by Frederick McGrath.

On summer Sundays a partition can be opened to greatly enlarge the sanctuary. In winter, the church can be smaller to accommodate the winter population. Masses vary according to the season as attendance requires.

Parish activities are carried on in connection with the mother church in Orleans.

Chapel of St. James the Fisherman (Episcopal)

ROUTE 6, WELLFLEET

Until 1957, vacationing Episcopal communicants met summers in the First Congregational Church of Wellfleet. Then the Carey E. Melville family gave a pine covered hill overlooking the Mid-Cape Highway, and this unusual chapel was built.

In name and design the building spans the Christian era, for St. James the Fisherman was one of Christ's first apostles. Also, his emblem--the scallop shells--is also that of the fishing village of Wellfleet and of this chapel. Architect Olaf Hammerstrom designed a contemporary building with interior beams that remind one of the ribs of a fishing vessel. The soaring bell tower thrusts the cross into the Cape sky for a beacon to fishermen and sailors.

The late Bishop James Pike, founding priest, conducted services here that were forerunners of liturgical renewal in modern day Christian worhip. Although there is seating for 200 people, no one is more than four seats away from the Holy Table, which is in the center of the building. Clergy, choir, and lay reader seats are with their families, making participation informal and natural. Thus though innovative and modern, services are also more primitive and ancient. The chapel is open for worship each summer from mid-June to mid-September and lay participation is encouraged.

First Congregational Church
(United Church of Christ)

MAIN STREET, WELLFLEET

The oldest church in Wellfleet, this was established before the town. The citizens of the area, which was then called Billingsgate, petitioned the mother church in Eastham for a separation. A small church was then built in the Taylor Hill area and the first service held July 29, 1723. Only an old burial ground now marks the spot.

In 1735 a larger church was built at the head of Duck Creek. Wellfleet became a separate town in 1763. Then a third church building was constructed at Duck Creek in 1829. It was used until 1850 when the congregation voted to build the present church on Main Street overlooking Wellfleet Harbor. The second site is also now marked only by a burial ground--the larger Duck Creek Cemetery.

The present building, of modified Greek Revival style, was designed by carpenter-architects, who used building materials from the old church. Originally this church had a steeple, but it blew down in 1879 and was replaced by a cupola. The three-faced town clock is unique. It strikes ship's time (nautical bells) instead of the conventional hours. There is a lovely old Hook and Hastings organ and an interesting old balcony. Though steeped in history, the church has an active parish endeavoring to show the church as "a believing and practising fellowship."

Our Lady of Lourdes Church (Catholic)

MAIN STREET, WELLFLEET

The first Catholic residents of this town were served by priests from Provincetown and Harwich in the mid-1850's. In 1874, when Provincetown was officially made a parish, Wellfleet was made its mission along with Truro and North Truro. They remained so until 1904 when the Fall River Diocese was formed and the three missions were returned to Harwich.

In 1911, Wellfleet was put under the charge of the Sacred Heart Fathers and Truro and North Truro were made its missions. This arrangement continues today.

The original chapel was built on Route 6 in 1900. It stood near the small Parish cemetery which is adjacent to the town cemetery. Then a new church was constructed in the center of the village after 1911.

The church was designed by the pastor and built by pastor and people. Though no one had previous experience, the building was cleverly and intricately constructed. The church seats about 300 and is joined to the Rectory by a connecting addition. The exterior is a pleasing mellow structure with colonial fan doorway and small tower.

Weekday activities are centered here as the parish seeks to serve its own members as well as the community.

Wellfleet Methodist Church

MAIN STREET, WELLFLEET

Methodism began in Wellfleet when an itinerant preacher gave his first sermon in 1797. The first Methodist class began with three women members. They met at first in private homes. During 1816-17 a building of traditional New England meetinghouse style was erected on the site of the Pleasant Hill cemetery.

The church was removed and rebuilt on the present site in 1842-43. It was larger, containing two galleries and 118 pews. This was remodeled again in 1863. Then it was struck by lightning on February 28, 1891, and burned to the ground.

With only $3,000 insurance money, the society heroically undertook the rebuilding for $8,800. The present church was dedicated January 26, 1892, with all bills paid.

Important has been the impact of this parish on the community and the world at large. Isaac Rich, one of the founders of Boston University, came from it as did Dr. Nehemiah Hopkins. The latter served as a medical missionary in China, founding the John L. Hopkins Memorial Hospital in Peking in honor of his brother who had pledged his life to mission work. Captain Lorenzo Dow Baker, of United Fruit Co., was for years a devoted member and benefactor.

Special features of the sanctuary are beautiful stained glass windows designed by artist Claire Leighton. A church school wing was added in 1971. Also, this was one of the two churches which helped launch the Fisherman's Players, a Methodist drama company. The church is now associated with the United Methodist Church in Provincetown.

First Congregational Church
(United Church of Christ)
TRURO CENTER

When Truro was constituted a town in 1709, it was with the stipulation that a meetinghouse be built within three years and a pastor called. Thus in 1711 John Avery was called as minister and a church was built in Pond Village. A second building was constructed in 1720 in North Truro. About a century later, in 1827, it was decided to build a new meetinghouse in Truro Center. The present edifice was built on land donated by the sea captain Freeman Atkins. It was to serve as a beacon for ships.

The new church cost $2,673.64 plus $320.00 for a bell from the Revere Foundry. Joseph Revere, son of Paul, cast the bell. In 1845 the vestry was constructed which shortened the sanctuary. Until nearby Union Hall was available in 1860, town meetings were held in the gallery of this church at the rate of $25.00 per year.

In the years 1955--1958 the church was restored. Swinging doors on the pews were rehung and the bell tower repaired and waterproofed. The old wallpaper, which had been on the walls for one hundred years, was reproduced by a special screen process. Windows, originally of Sandwich glass, were repaired. In this lovely old sanctuary in a town full of seafarers an interesting touch is that the window catches were made in the shape of whales.

Sacred Heart Church (Catholic)
TRURO CENTER

As early as 1860, Catholics in this town were served by visiting priests from Sandwich, Harwich, and Provincetown in that order. Then, in 1874, it officially became a mission of Provincetown, when the latter was designated a parish.

With the organization of the Fall River Diocese, this church was attached to the Harwich parish. Finally, in 1911, the Truro Center church was assigned to Wellfleet when it became a parish. It continues so today and is staffed by Sacred Heart Fathers.

The church building was constructed in 1895. The pastor purchased an old skating rink in South Truro and used the lumber for the new church. The building is a pleasing small structure just off Route 6 at the beginning of the Hill of Churches.

A Saturday night Mass is scheduled throughout the winter, with more Masses added when warm weather comes. Parish activity centers in Wellfleet and Confraternity of Christian Doctrine classes are held in North Truro church.

Christian Union Church

ROUTE 6A, NORTH TRURO

The last of the 18th Century, Methodist itinerants preached in North Truro (then called Pond Village) in a circuit that included Provincetown and Truro Center. The first organization recorded, however, was in 1822, when a class of twenty was formed. After a few years, these members joined those at Truro Center in building a meetinghouse in the latter place. This remained the church home of both Societies for 14 years. About 1834 a Sabbath School was organized, each member being taxed.

In 1840, the Methodists of North Truro withdrew and united with Congregationalists in building the present Union church. The building was erected by local workmen entirely. About 1875 the building was raised and a vestry placed beneath. In 1885 a parsonage was purchased.

The parish currently maintains a vigorous community outreach, with the Messenger newsletter and visitation of the sick. There is an exterior redecoration program being planned for the interesting old meetinghouse.

Our Lady of Perpetual Help Church (Catholic)

OFF ROUTE 6A, NORTH TRURO

Just south of Route 6A in this village is a small frame church that has served Catholics in this area since the turn of the century. It is a mission of Our Lady of Lourdes Church in Wellfleet and is staffed by Sacred Heart Fathers from that parish.

In the late 1800's Catholics were served at various times by visiting priests from Sandwich, Harwich, and Provincetown and services were held in homes. The mission was first attached to Provincetown in 1874, Harwich in 1904, and finally assigned to Wellfleet in 1911.

The interesting small church is noted for its stained-glass windows which somewhat resemble those done by Tiffany. Confraternity of Christian Doctrine classes are held here for children of Truro Center as well as those in North Truro. Other activities center at the Wellfleet church. Services are held here Sunday morning in the winter, with more services added in summertime.

United Methodist Church
SHANK PAINTER ROAD, PROVINCETOWN

The next vessel of importance arriving in Provincetown after the "Mayflower" according to Methodists, was the vessel of Captain William Humbert, which put into the harbor in 1793 because of adverse winds. Each night the Captain, who was a Methodist preacher, came ashore and spoke. The seed took root and by 1795 a class was organized. At one time there were eleven such classes meeting in the township.

There was much local opposition at first, but the members persisted and a building was erected. It was called the Old Oak Meetinghouse and stood on Winthrop Street. Eventually the parish flourished so well that three-quarters of the townspeople were Methodists. There were three buildings that preceeded Centre Church, the beautiful structure with the graceful steeple that housed Methodists until recent years.

In the fall of 1847 a few prominent Society members felt there should be a church in the west end of town. They organized and purchased the old Universalist Society building in 1848, forming Wesley Chapel. In 1865, this congregation erected a new building which was called Centenary Church.

About the year 1945 Centenary and Centre Churches merged, using Centre Church building. Then in 1960 the members built the present contemporary structure pictured above. Centre Church was sold and became an Art Museum.

A Church School building, offices, and Fellowship Hall and Sanctuary make up the church plant which serves an active parish, now associated with the Wellfleet Methodist Church.

Church of St. Peter the Apostle (Catholic)

11 PRINCE STREET, PROVINCETOWN

When a few Catholic families were numbered among the townsfolk in 1852, Rev. Joseph Finotti was sent by the Bishop in Boston to serve a mission in Provincetown. After arriving on August 26th, he heard confessions at Pilgrim House and the next day celebrated Mass in a private home. Of the 70 who attended, the majority were Irish, most of the Portuguese arriving later on the Cape.

Regular visits followed by Father Finotti and other priests. Though a Catholic Parish House was purchased in 1854 and another hall leased later, a church was not built and dedicated until 1874. The *Provincetown Advocate* reports the seating capacity 600, and the frescoing work "highly creditable."

At first St. Peter was a mission of Harwich, but soon had Truro and Wellfleet church as missions of its own. Until 1904 Mass was celebrated in private homes then chapels were built in Truro in 1895 and Wellfleet in 1900. Meanwhile the Provincetown Parish grew. In November of 1878 a devotion of forty hours culminated in the confirmation of over 200 youth and adults.

In 1886, a new Rectory was built beside the church and a bell was installed in the church in 1887. In 1914 the Sanctuary was extended and new windows installed. An exceptionally fine mural by Eugene Sparks of St. Peter walking on the sea enriches the Sanctuary.

The Universalist Church of Provincetown

COMMERCIAL STREET, PROVINCETOWN

In 1820, Sylvia and Elizabeth Freeman, who lived on the spit of sand forming the Cape tip, retrieved a black object from the surf. It was a book entitled "The Life of Rev. John Murray--Preacher of Universal Salvation." Read by many, it was instrumental in the founding of this church in 1829.

The first small chapel on Commercial Street was used for about twenty years. Then it was replaced with the present impressive structure. When it was dedicated in December of 1847, it was named the Church of the Redeemer, Universalist, but was later changed to The Universalist Church of Provincetown.

The elaborate three-stage steeple in classic Greek Revival style is a striking feature of the building. Carl Wendle, a young German artist, painted the interior walls of the Sanctuary with "Trompe L'Oeil" (egg tempera), giving a pillared and vaulted effect. There is an illusionary apse as well as a coffered dome and Corinthian pilasters. The crystal chandelier originally burned sperm whale oil at $1.25 a gallon. Globes were originally of Sandwich glass.

The small but active membership is enlarged by tourists in summer. The thrift shop makes available new and nearly-new clothing and articles. The church is a member of the Unitarian-Universalist Association, and its building was placed on the National Register of Historic Places in 1972.

Church of St. Mary of the Harbor (Episcopal)

519 COMMERCIAL STREET, PROVINCETOWN

In 1904, a few devout Episcopalians began plans for their own place of worship in Provincetown. Fifteen years later, in 1919, they were able to purchase a sturdy old "salt house" on a superb waterfront location. The top stories of the fine old building were removed and the remainder became the church. Later, the old Sand Bar Club in the west end was taken apart piece by piece and moved to the site to form the Chancel, while the original house became the Nave. Frederick Waugh, famous marine painter, drew the plans and Rev. Robert Wood Nicholson, first year-round priest to serve the small Mission, developed the lovely Church Garden.

During the early 1930's a circle of world famous artists - painters - and sculptors began to add to the beauty of the structure by giving their works in memory of loved ones. The church was dedicated in August of 1936.

In the garden is the S-4 Cross, placed there in memory of the men who lost their lives in the disaster of December 17, 1927, when the S-4 was rammed and sunk off Race Point. A broken circle of metal at the base of the cross is part of the sealing ring from the S-4 conning tower brought up in the net of a fisherman and placed with the cross.

Its busy parish life of service to church members and community has as its background an unusual building "with a sense of harmony and proportion which makes it an oasis of peace, even during bustling summer days."

Holy Redeemer Church (Catholic)

HIGHLAND AVENUE, CHATHAM

Land was purchased and the ground was broken for Holy Redeemer Church on November 30, 1915. On August 27, 1916, the new building was dedicated by the Most Rev. Daniel F. Feehan, D.D., Bishop of Fall River.

In early days Holy Redeemer operated as a mission attached first to the parish in Wellfleet and then to Holy Trinity in West Harwich. The children were taught catechism in their homes by their parents and later they met in the house on Highland Avenue which is now the Rectory.

During the years the small mission grew and the increasing number of summer residents and visitors made it necessary to enlarge the church. Ground was broken in December of 1953, and the first Mass celebrated there in early June, 1954. The Church was re-dedicated on July 21, 1954, by the Most Rev. James L. Connolly, D.D., Bishop of Fall River.

In recent years the mission church Our Lady of Grace was built as this church's mission. In addition to the two church buildings and the Rectory, there is a C.C.D. Center located next to the Holy Redeemer Church. Here grades one through twelve are taught religion--both the fundamental concepts of Catholic faith and religion as it applies to daily living.

Other organizations are the Parish Council, Association of Sacred Hearts, Holy Redeemer Guild, and St. Vincent de Paul Society. Each group contributes to parish life and to the needs in the local community and elsewhere.

First Congregational Church
(United Church of Christ)

CORNER MAIN STREET AND OLD HARBOR ROAD, CHATHAM

Chatham's first settler, William Nickerson, held services in his home and gave religious instruction during his life time. The nearest church was then in Eastham. In 1679, Plymouth Colony Court ordered the inhabitants of Monomoyick (the Indian name for Chatham) "to raise among themselves five pounds a year in money and other substantial goods and deposit it in the hands of some faithful person to be kept in stocke towards the inabling of them to build a meeting house or a house for a minnester." By 1693, there was a church because the town voted to repair it.

In 1700, a church was built just west of Great Hill in the part of the cemetery where the oldest graves are found. This was replaced with another structure in 1729. In 1720, the church was officially formed with seven male members. Until 1824, the church was supported by taxes. On August 9 of that year, town support ceased and the members agreed to raise the money needed.

The present building was erected in 1830 on the site now known as Union Cemetery. The church was moved to its present location and remodeled in 1866. A new Parish House was built in 1961. That same year the church became part of the United Church of Christ. In 1968 a Chancel was added to the Sanctuary. Antique whale oil lamps and an impressive old chandelier beautify the interior. A variety of organizations serve all ages and provide channels for service in the parish and beyond.

First United Methodist Church

17 CROSS STREET, CHATHAM

The roots of this church go back to 1799 when an itinerant Methodist preacher visited the town. The first official class was formed, however, in 1816. The first meetinghouse, a rough log structure, was built in 1820. "Wonderful and glorious were the manifestations of God's power and grace in that old house" says the record.

A second edifice, a more refined structure, was built in 1833. It was located near what is now Seaside Cemetery. It was later sold and moved, to become the town almshouse. After that, it became a guest house, was then purchased by the Roman Catholic Church. It was demolished in 1969.

The present building was constructed in 1849 and underwent major renovations in 1900. These included installation of Belgian and Tiffany stained-glass windows. The Marcellus Eldridges gave most of these in memory of their parents. Within a few houses of each other, and before the work was completed, the Eldridges passed away. A niece had the central windows done as a memorial to them.

This large and active congregation is part of the Chatham-Harwich United Methodist Parish.

St. Christopher's Church (Episcopal)

MAIN STREET, CHATHAM

The beginnings of this church were in the fall of 1960 when parishioners of the Church of the Holy Spirit in Orleans felt the need for an Episopal church in Chatham. With the help of dedicated laymen, and the aid and encouragement of clergy, services were begun in the Chatham Post American Legion Hall. Then members rented and in 1961 purchased the former Universalist Church. On May 1, 1963, it became a mission.

The church building was erected around 1880 and contains a Stephens tracker organ about 130 years old. In 1962 the church was completely redone with new chancel, kneelers, lighting, and heat added. Parish status was reached in 1967.

Land adjacent to the church was purchased in 1969 and later converted to a park. Then in 1971, when more space was needed, a new Parish House was added containing, among other things, offices, Rector's study, and Sacristy. The Rectory is on Old Harbor Road.

Currently the Sanctuary is being redone under the direction of Rev. Edward West, Canon of the Cathedral of St. John the Divine in New York City, one of the country's foremost liturgical experts.

The church members are cognizant of needs beyond the parish. When a large bequest was left to the church in 1971, it was placed in a Charitable Trust. The income, which exceeds $7,000 each year, is given for charitable purposes outside the parish and is above the quota for missions assigned by the Diocese.

First Church of Christ, Scientist

MAIN STREET, CHATHAM

Christian Scientists first met in Chatham in 1885, it is said, but no formal organization resulted. Then in February of 1946 a group met together again and held services in the Masonic Hall. In March of that year a Society was formed. By November, it was recognized as such by the Mother Church in Boston.

From 1947 to 1958, the members met in the building then belonging to the Universalist Church. During that period, in 1952, it became officially a church, known as First Church of Christ, Scientist.

According to official records, ground was broken for the new church in March of 1958. This imposing structure faces travelers as they enter Chatham, coming east on Route 28. The four columns form an impressive portico over the main entrance. It was dedicated September 8, 1963.

The parish sponsors a reading room on the Main Street of the town and holds midweek testimonial meetings in addition to Sunday Church and Sunday School sessions.

Our Lady of Grace (Catholic)

ROUTES 28 and 137, SOUTH CHATHAM

This beautiful modern church was built in 1963 in South Chatham. Known as Our Lady of Grace, the Church is part of the parish of the Holy Redeemer Church in Chatham. Though it is only open during June, July, August, and early September, it is filled to capacity at all Masses due to the number of summer visitors.

This interesting structure sits on a knoll at a strategic Cape Cod intersection. Its dramatic steeple is a landmark for quite a distance. The building is of wood and seats approximately 400 people. Recesses each side of the altar allow for extra seating. This is a popular place for parents with children, for they are so close to the celebration of the Mass.

Church furnishings were contributed by parish families and many are memorials. The entire altar is covered with gold carpeting, which gives a feeling of spaciousness to the worshipful interior.

South Chatham Community Church

MAIN STREET, SOUTH CHATHAM

In the early part of this century, the people of South Chatham recognized the need of a religious foundation. Consequently the Bethel Society, a religious activity, was formed on September 7, 1910. Phoebe Emery gave land for a building. This first meeting place was destroyed by fire in 1915.

The Ladies Circle of Industry then conveyed another building on the premises to the Bethel Society. More space was needed in recent years, and a two-story addition containing classrooms was completed in December of 1959.

Through most of its early history the Society shared ministers with various nearby Methodist churches. Some felt, however, that a non-denominational church should be formed. Thus on April 28, 1969, incorporators met to form the South Chatham Community Church. In February of 1971 a full-time minister was called.

The interesting white frame building, with its square tower and minute steeple, stands adjacent to the library and the Village Hall. It's just the right location for a church whose slogan is "a neighborhood church for a neighborly people."

West Chatham Christadelphian Ecclesia

ROUTE 28, SOUTH CHATHAM

Christadelphians began meeting in Chatham when Brother Seabury and Sister Priscilla Gibbs came from Brockton and later from Cataumet to teach Bible classes, being faithful regardless of the weather. The first members were part of the Christadelphians in Cataumet. On May 18, 1939, they voted to form their own group. Services were held from June 1939 to January 1957 in Circle Hall in West Chatham. Then Memorial Services were moved to the Village Hall in South Chatham.

Each Sunday morning services are held in the Village Hall, while weekly Bible classes are held in homes on week nights. Serving or arranging bretheren are the officers and these men take turns in presiding at the Memorial Services. This ecclesia, like all others, is autonomous, having only a fraternal connection with other ecclesias. Representatives meet with other ecclesias occasionally for conferences.

South Harwich United Methodist Church

CHATHAM ROAD, SOUTH HARWICH

Originally this parish was organized as a Reformed Methodist church in the late 1700's. The members worshipped in earlier buildings, then erected this church in 1836.

In 1845 the church members changed the name to Wesleyan Methodist, then in August of 1854 changed the name again to Methodist Episcopal Church. The property was then deeded to the Methodist Episcopal Conference.

The building has remained the same through the years except for minor improvements which include the removal of a balcony and the installation of electricity. It is a pleasing white frame building, set amid an old cemetery.

The church is now part of the Chatham-Harwich United Methodist Parish.

United Methodist Church

ROUTE 137, EAST HARWICH

This is one of the oldest Methodist churches on the Cape, for Jessie Lee, famous itinerant preacher, spoke here. Regular services began in 1797. The first meetinghouse was built in 1799 and such was the prosperity of the society that twelve years later the building was too small.

The present spacious structure, surrounded by an ancient graveyard, was then built. It was dedicated on January 1, 1812. By 1848 the building needed repairing and remodeling, after which it was rededicated. The first Sabbath School began in 1845. The church was remodeled again in 1906.

When the membership became smaller, the church was connected with the Methodist church in South Harwich. Now these two and the Chatham Methodist Church form the Chatham-Harwich United Methodist Parish. The building serves as part of the outreach of the United Parish, housing Headstart among other community organizations.

Jehovah's Witnesses Kingdom Hall

PLEASANT BAY ROAD, HARWICH

There were Jehovah's Witnesses on Cape Cod prior to World War I. They met in Circle Hall in South Harwich in the early years. Then in 1958 members built Kingdom Hall in East Harwich. The structure is built to fit architecturally into the Cape Cod area. It has been remodeled three times, most recently in 1973 when the seating capacity was increased. Exterior refurbishing and landscaping are currently planned. Kingdom Halls are kept simple, so the congregation will be emphasized rather than a building.

The congregation's prime ministry is a door-to-door educational work of teaching, preaching, and Bible study. In addition, a minimum of five hours a week are devoted by members to Bible study, ministry school, and educational concerns.

Headquarters for this and other congregations is in Brooklyn, New York, home of the Watchtower Bible and Tract Society.

Christ Church (Episcopal)

MAIN STREET, HARWICH PORT

Although earlier services were known to have been held, the first records indicate that Episcopal services were held in a Social Hall in Chatham in 1914. These led to the establishing of Christ Church. When the original hall, now no longer standing, became inadequate, services were moved to the Satucket Building and later to the East Livingroom of the Snow Inn.

A gift of $5,000 in 1925 began the drive for the present church building which was erected on the main thoroughfare. First services were held in 1926. These were summer services only for many years, with guest preachers officiating.

In 1954 the parish decided to have services year round and the ladies of Christ Church Guild provided money for a heating plant. The parish grew and a Parish House was added in 1958. Facilities included classrooms, Parish Hall, and kitchen. By 1966 another addition was needed, so a Church School Chapel and more classrooms were built. Membership has continued to grow, doubling in the last decade.

An active parish produces many projects and organizations. This church is no exception. Projects are largely for missions, with special interest in the Philippines.

Pilgrim Congregational Church
(United Church of Christ)
ROUTE 28, HARWICH PORT

Early records of the Pilgrim Church Society go back to 1854 when some citizens felt the importance of "maintaining and supporting the Gospel in its purity." It was agreed from the beginning that "in all conferences and prayer meetings, females have an equal right to speak and pray."

On January 16, 1855, application was made to the Commonwealth for permission to organize and the meetinghouse was dedicated February 1, 1855, when also the first pastor was called. In the same year a clock was purchased for the tower "much to the enjoyment of the village." A church bell was installed in July 1859. Also that year the records show "the sexton must be careful of the sweeping and dusting of God's House."

In 1956, a Parish House was constructed containing classrooms, kitchen, recreation room, assembly hall, and memorial parlor. A Chapel was built and dedicated in 1966 and is used for overflow congregations, small weddings, baptisms, and funerals. In 1965, a new Chancel was installed and a memorial stained glass window. A two-manual 1300 pipe organ was installed in 1966 and a carillon in 1972.

Though parishioners are proud of their heritage, they are also conscious of future service to parish and wider community through committees and clubs. These include mission and education projects, a large library to promote good reading, and musical emphasis.

Holy Trinity Catholic Church

MAIN STREET, WEST HARWICH

Pleasant Lake Avenue was the site of the first Roman Catholic church in town. This second Cape parish was created a mission in 1866, largely through the efforts of Patrick Drum. George Swift was the builder of the first church, which was a white wooden building with a tower. The first mass was celebrated in July of 1866. In 1869 this became a full parish, with responsibility for the territory to Provincetown. Rev. Cornelius O'Connor traveled throughout the area to say mass and solemnize the sacraments.

In December 1927, the church burned and the parish relocated to West Harwich. A second church was built where the present building now stands. The second edifice was destroyed by fire in the year 1963. Through the years it has had several missions, but in recent years is responsible for Our Lady of Annunciation in Dennisport.

A modern new church was completed and dedicated in 1965. The plant includes an educational building which once was a parochial school staffed by the Sisters of Mercy. Currently it is used for catechism classes. The new church is of pleasing design and a "sense of splendor is felt as one enters."

First Congregational Church
(United Church of Christ)

MAIN STREET, HARWICH

In 1744, Harwich Center residents, tired of traveling to the North Precinct (now Brewster) asked to have worship in their own neighborhood. This was approved by the General Court in 1747. Samuel Nickerson and Benjamin Smalley gave the land where the present church stands and the church was officially organized in 1747.

The first church was built just west of the present edifice with the parsonage nearby. In 1791, a second building was erected for $1,219. This had square pews, galleries, a pulpit with sounding board, and deacon's benches. The third meetinghouse was erected in 1832 and is the nucleus of the present building. Boston architect J. D. Towle, renovated it in 1854. A steeple 100 feet tall was added. The church was legally incorporated in 1896.

In 1881, the church ladies erected a chapel, which in the renovation of 1954 became the present Parish House. Across the street is Broadbrooks, given for a parsonage, but which is now the Church Office Building. The modern parsonage is on Beriah Brooks Road. Currently an 1896 Hutchings organ is being installed in the sanctuary.

Throughout its history this church has "sought to be a community of people that rejoices in its heritage of faith, celebrates the gospel, welcomes diversity, practises brotherhood, promotes justice, deepens spiritual life, shares with others and remains open to fresh disclosures of God's word in our time."

First Baptist Church of West Harwich and Dennisport

ROUTE 28, WEST HARWICH

The Great Awakening under Jonathan Edwards and George Whitfield was responsible for the beginnings of this church, when "the Baptist Church in Harwich was constituted in 1757, embracing seventy-two members." The actual day was September 29th and location was the northwest part of town. This is the oldest Baptist Fellowship in the county. The first meetinghouse was erected on land now occupied as a cemetery in North Harwich about 1760. In 1804, a larger house was erected just south of the earlier building.

In the years between 1823 and 1826, one hundred and sixty members left the church to found Baptist churches in Brewster, Chatham, and Orleans. In later years, the Evangelical Baptist Church in South Yarmouth and the Calvary Baptist originated from this church.

The meetinghouse was raised and moved to its present location in the 1870's, so it would be nearer the center of population. At this time a Hook and Hastings tracker organ was installed and the interior was improved and renovated. The six large stained-glass windows in the main sanctuary and the five in front were given by Job Chase, of Chase and Sanborn Co. Many other memorials testify to the concern and commitment of parishioners through the years, symbolic of the church's slogan, "A Spiritual Lighthouse on Cape Cod."

First Church of Christ Scientist

648 MAIN STREET, HARWICH PORT

In 1954, a Christian Science Society was formed in this town, by 1960 becoming a branch of the Mother Church, First Church of Christ, Scientist, in Boston.

The building is located on Route 28 overlooking beautiful Wychmere Harbor. Open year round, there are Sunday services, Sunday School, and Wednesday evening meetings.

Projects include a reading room at 560A Main Street, where Christian Science publications are available. Free lectures are sponsored twice a year. Literature is made available in commercial locations, and services are held in correctional institutions and elsewhere when requested.

Our Lady of Annunciation Church
(CATHOLIC)

UPPER COUNTY ROAD, DENNISPORT

This interesting church was built in the spring of 1953 to meet the needs of the expanding population in the Dennisport area. The first mass was offered here on July 5, 1953, and the mission was dedicated by The Most Reverend Bishop Connolly on July 16th of that year. His coat of arms hangs above the front door.

When crowded conditions prevailed, an extension to the building was added in 1970. This new area serves as a youth and social center from September to May and augments the space in the main church in the summer. It is a mission of Holy Trinity Catholic Church in West Harwich.

Cape Cod Pentacostal Assembly

MILL STREET, DENNISPORT

The beginnings of this church go back several decades to meetings held in South Yarmouth at the old Kelly Chapel on Olde Main Street. These were the first Pentecostal meetings held on the Cape. In 1931, the church was officially organized, Shortly after, members bought land in Dennisport and the present church was built. Help was given on construction by three men from the Gospel Tabernacle of the Zion Bible Institute in East Providence.

In the early 1950's, the basement area under the auditorium was made into a chapel and church school rooms, then about 1971 the auditorium was redecorated.

The church is an independent one, though it has fellowship with other churches. Decisions are made by the Board of the Church. Services are informal, with singing and testimonies and many youth attend. Some of the outreach includes visiting in nursing homes, street services in summer, beach work among youth, and Bible classes for children.

Reorganized Church of Jesus Christ of Latter Day Saints

SEA STREET, DENNISPORT

In the 1830's this congregation was formed when adherents of Joseph Smith brought word of the new Mormon church. After the founder's death and Brigham Young led the members west in 1847, some Cape families joined the exodus. Many church members remained in the midwest, eventually forming the Reorganized church with Joseph's son as president. This church joined with them in 1868. Headquarters for the Southern New England Conference is Lexington, while the home of the National organization is in Independence, Missouri.

The Cape type frame church building was erected about 1870. An addition is currently in progress, giving space for the Sunday School large meetings and dining facilities. The Zionist group for children and Helping Hand Society for women are vehicles for parish work.

The Dennisport Church of the Nazarene

CROSS AND DEPOT STREETS, DENNISPORT

On June 23, 1906, this church was organized out of a concern for preserving the Holiness Movement, which followed the precepts of John Wesley's early Methodist teaching. Under the leadership of their first minister and during its early years, it grew from twelve to forty members and often there was standing room only in the small wooden frame building. The parish was a mission of the Nazarene Denomination and in intervening years has been served by a series of supply ministers.

Though it would have been easy to let the doors close when it struggled for existence, loyal devoted laymen and women determined to "keep the church open for the good of all and the glory of God." In May of 1960 the church merged with the parish in West Harwich and the present church building was constructed. By 1964, a small nucleus of the faithful, with a full-time pastor again, became a permanent church, no longer a mission.

In 1973 work began on an addition, with completion in 1974. The sanctuary was doubled in size, and classrooms, Nursery, Pastor's Study, and Fellowship Hall are included. The church has a mission outreach and emphasizes Bible study groups for adults and youth. It is a "little church with a big heart--a church whose people care."

Congregational Church of South Dennis
(United Church of Christ)
218 MAIN STREET, SOUTH DENNIS

On a knoll surrounded by an ancient graveyard stands this old white church built in 1835. It is also known as "The Captains' Church" and is the second building on this site. Though services were held in the village as early as 1765, the first meetinghouse was not built until 1795. In 1817, the church became independent of the parish on the northside and incorporated. Its official organization dates from June of 1817. South of the present structure and graveyard is the 200-year-old parsonage. Originally a small Cape half house, it has had several additions through the years. The adjacent modern Parish House was built in 1966.

The historic church sanctuary has many unique furnishings including the pews from the original building. On the west wall are two tablets perpetuating the names of 102 sea captains, most of whom were in this parish. The rosewood organ was built in 1762 by John Snetzler and is reputed to be the oldest pipe organ in continual use in America. On the east wall is a 6' by 10' mural of the *Adoration* by the artist Edwin Howland Blashfield. The stately chandelier has old whale oil vessels and delicately etched Sandwich glass globes.

The church is more than a museum, however, for there is a steady stream of faithful parishioners of all ages through its buildings. The Union Circle, assisted by the Men's Club, operates a summer Thrift Shop in Liberty Hall, which makes goods and clothing available at minimal cost and augments missionary giving. The church also sponsors meetings when contemporary issues are explored in the context of faith.

West Dennis Community Church
(United Church of Christ)

MAIN STREET (ROUTE 28), WEST DENNIS

Services began in this village in 1825 when converts, resulting from visits of itinerant Methodist preachers, met in homes and in the school. In 1833-1834 a Church and Society were organized as part of the Wesleyan Church. A small meetinghouse was erected on the present site.

In 1848 the church was flourishing and needed more space, so the church was sawed in half. One section was moved north and new construction added between the two sections. A steeple was built and provision was made for a church clock and bell to be "purchased and installed when funds were available." This happy day came in 1856 when a celebration marked the arrival of a bell marked "cast in 1854 by Henry Hooper and Co., Boston." The clock was also manufactured in Boston by the Howard and Davis Company.

In 1873 the church affiliated with the Methodist Episcopal Church. Numerous improvements, including stained glass windows, the present pews, and a vestry were added by 1897. In 1935, a Centennial Celebration was held. The church left the Methodist fold in 1946 and joined with the Community Church movement.

In 1959 the church joined Barnstable Association which is part of the United Church of Christ, though it retained its name of Community Church. Major remodeling in recent years included the addition of a new Parish House, a Youth Acitivity Center, and replacing the old steeple, which badly needed repair. Two of the major emphases of this active parish are toward youth and elderly people.

United Methodist Church

322 MAIN STREET, SOUTH YARMOUTH

The Methodist Society of this town was organized in the 1840's and met in a building in the old graveyard on Willow Street in the Bass River section. When it was voted to build a new church, in 1852 the sanctuary of the present church was erected on this site. The cost of $2,000 was raised by selling shares at $25 each.

Members were joined by people from the Methodist Church in North Harwich about 1900 when that church was closed. The Harwich church had been in existence since 1842.

In 1883, Elisha Taylor gave money to build a vestry onto the church, and the chapel was named for him. Then in the early 1950's the three-floor parish hall was built.

In this era, the church bell was used as a fire alarm and as a signal for other disasters as well as to summon the faithful to church.

Fishermen's House was purchased in 1969. This provides additional space for expanded ministries to the community, which include an ecumenically-sponsored vacation school. Study groups and prayer groups augment the usual programs. Worldwide as well as local missionary projects are supported by this growing parish.

St. David's Episcopal Church

OLD MAIN STREET, SOUTH YARMOUTH

Following a survey by the Episcopal Diocese of Massachusetts in the Cape Cod area, St. David's Episcopal Church was established in South Yarmouth in January of 1966. Approximately 30 families were present at the first organizational meeting of this mission church in the Yarmouth Town Hall. First services were conducted January 23, 1966.

In February 1969, ground was broken for a church building in the present location. The following December 21st the first worship service was held in the new church. The building is of simple contemporary design with wooden shingles, plain glass windows (to bring the outdoors inside), and surrounded by an enclosed flower garden. It also has an open Memorial Churchyard. Inside, the feeling is of openness and simplicity. The focal point is the magnificent free standing altar.

The church presently has an active, dedicated group of about 250 families. Parish status is slated for 1974. Through the usual organizations and services the church ministers to the surrounding commmunity. It assists with such worthy projects as Head Start, as well as making toys and clothing for those in need.

Bass River Community Baptist Church
(AMERICAN BAPTIST)

OLD MAIN STREET AND WOOD ROAD, SOUTH YARMOUTH

After twenty-six years at sea, Captain Simeon Crowell came home to stay and organized the First Baptist Church in Yarmouth in 1824. The Captain then gave the land for a church building and, after becoming ordained, became the first pastor. In 1826 a meetinghouse was erected, paid for by Captain Freeman Baker. It was so plain it was sometimes referred to as "The Lord's Barn." There was no belfry or steeple, no paint outside or in, and the pulpit was long and box-like. A melodeon was used for music and tallow candles provided light.

In 1860 the building was turned around, an extension was built at the rear and a belfry, steeple, and bell added. In 1893 the building was raised and a vestry built underneath. The year 1914 saw the steeple blow down. It rested on the floor in front of the pulpit. Later, the steeple was replaced at a cost of $300. The Baptist Cemetery Association was formed in 1916.

The name of the church was changed to Bass River Community Church in 1949. Around 1952 a parsonage was built and a Fellowship Hall added. Both of these are on Wood Road, behind the church. The Fellowship Hall, which houses parish activities, was a converted mess hall from Otis Air Force Base. For many years the parish shared a minister with other nearby Baptist churches. Now it has a full-time pastor, and parishioners are active in community and mission endeavors.

South Yarmouth Friends Meeting

NORTH MAIN STREET, SOUTH YARMOUTH

Once so many residents of South Yarmouth belonged to this Friends Meeting that the town was called Quaker Village. The first Quakers came to the Cape from England and their visits resulted in permanent meetings in Sandwich and Yarmouth. The latter dates from 1659 when the first Friend moved here from Sandwich. At first meetings were held by him weekly, alone until neighbors joined in. Then a meetinghouse was erected on Follen's Pond, farther up the Bass River than this present one. A sign and visible boundaries of the burying ground still mark the first site.

This present meetinghouse dates from 1809. It is consistent with the Quaker belief in simplicity. There is a partition to divide the sexes when separate business meetings were held. Outside there is a burial ground where markers are of uniform size and there are no epitaphs. The Friends believe "death is the great leveler, imposing democracy on us all." Quaker names like Thankful and Experience abound.

Services are held here each Sunday. Beyond the graveyard is the schoolhouse which was moved from a nearby site and serves as a parish hall. This Friends meeting is a preparative meeting, part of the Sandwich Monthly Meeting, the New Bedford Quarterly Meeting, and the New England Yearly Meeting. Friends have educational and political concerns and support the Friends Service Committee.

St. Pius The Tenth Catholic Church

STATION AVENUE, SOUTH YARMOUTH

Until fairly recently Catholics in this community attended church in Hyannis. Then a white church was built and a parish created in 1954. Dedication day was August 18, 1954.

Soon the parish outgrew the building and the present contemporary structure was begun in 1967 near the original church. The striking new church was dedicated June 12, 1969. It is cruciform in plan and magnificently appointed. The stained glass in the front is an unusual feature.

The former church was changed to a catechetical center. A handsome rectory on the grounds completes a fine church plant.

When the parish was created, it was given the responsibility for the mission, Our Lady of the Highway in Bass River.

Our Lady of the Highway (Catholic)

ROUTE 28, BASS RIVER

This summer church was originally a mission of St. Francis Xavier Church in Hyannis, but was transferred to St. Pius the Tenth Catholic Church when the latter was created a parish in 1954.

The church, designed by Earle Kempton, is in classic revival style simplified to fit the area. Erected in the summer of 1948, it was enlarged again in 1960. The altar is in the center of the church, which is overflowing with summer residents when it is opened for the warm months of the year.

Baha'i World Faith

The Baha'i faith came to Cape Cod in 1952 when a teacher arrived in Falmouth. A group soon began meeting regularly in homes and in 1961 a Spiritual Assembly was formed. The teaching spread further and a group was formed in Hyannis. A Spiritual Assembly resulted in 1972 for the Town of Barnstable. At present there are Baha'i groups meeting in South Yarmouth, Harwich, Dennis, Truro, and Provincetown.

The word "Baha'i" means follower of Bahaullah, who was founder of the Baha'i World Faith. This started in Persia in 1844 and now has spread to more than 300 countries and territories of the world. People of all races find here unity, equality, world mindedness, and truth. The World Shrine of the Bab is a magnificent golden-domed structure in Haifa, Israel. The national House of Worship is an intricately beautiful structure in Wilmette, Illinois.

Cape Baha'is meet in homes every nineteen days for religious services or feasts. Fireside meetings and those held in public halls are held to inform people of the Baha'i faith and teachings.

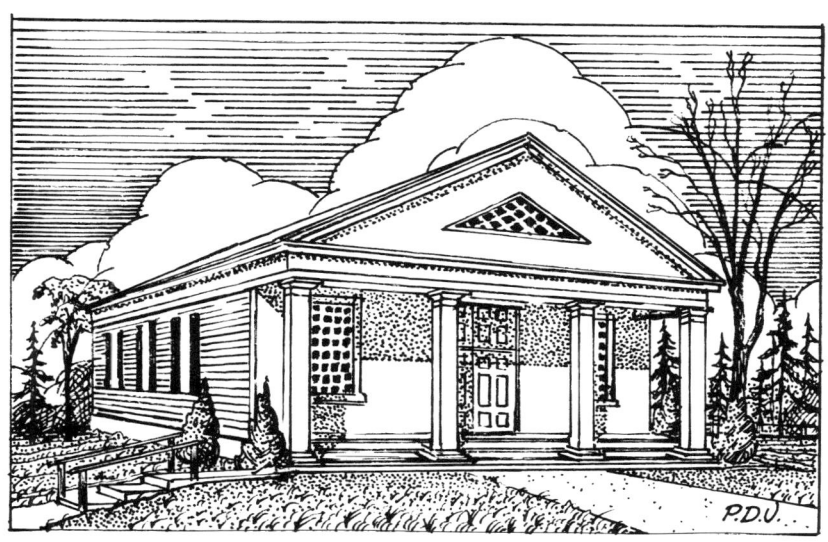

Evangelical Baptist Church

ROUTE 28 at POND STREET, SOUTH YARMOUTH

On January 14, 1960, a group of people met to discuss plans for a Baptist church and the outgrowth was the Evangelical Baptist Fellowship. First services were held in the Yarmouth Town Hall on February 7, 1960. By April it was officially constituted a church with forty-two charter members. It was incorporated later, on April 28, 1961.

In March of 1961, members purchased an acre of land which included also a seven-room house. Building plans were begun for a church on this property facing Route 28. On June 17, 1962, there was a ground-breaking ceremony. In an unusual observance, the congregation, led by the minister, pulled a plow across the turf. The two furrows resulting, formed the shape of a cross. This symbolized the joint effort of pastor and people in constructing a church and a fellowship.

First services were held in the new colonial-type building in April of 1963, on Easter Sunday. The architect was Gordon Robb and Tauno Karniala was contractor. Facilities include sanctuary, activities room, classrooms, offices, and choir room. A fiberglass Baptistry was installed in the chancel platform.

The church is connected with the Baptist General Conference of New England. Organizations include Women's Missionary Society, Boys Stockade, Girls Meeting God, Junior and Senior High Youth groups, as well as an Adult Fellowship and a College and Career group.

West Yarmouth Congregational Church
(United Church of Christ)

MAIN STREET (ROUTE 28), WEST YARMOUTH

The present church was organized September 30, 1840, by sixty-four members of The First Congregational Church of Yarmouth. Since it was necessary to walk or travel by ox-cart to services, parishioners on the south side of the Cape felt the need of their own church.

In 1794 the first building was constructed on the site of the present day West Yarmouth Post Office -- on Route 28 facing South Sea Street. A second and more modern building was erected in 1835. It had the horse sheds characteristic of church buildings of that era. In 1847 the South Evangelical Society came into being to have oversight of the business affairs of the church.

On November 30, 1907, the church building was moved west on Route 28 to its present location. Services were resumed in the building in March of 1908. In recent years an extensive building program was undertaken which included offices, classrooms, dining room, and a lounge. These and other renovations were completed in 1964.

Present day activities include groups for all ages within the parish and outreach to community organizations. Cooperation with the Council of Churches and support of mission work is stressed. The planning for the Nursing Home Visitor Program of Church Women United was begun here.

New Testament Baptist Church

HIGGINS CROWELL ROAD, WEST YARMOUTH

One of the most recent on Cape Cod, this church was started unofficially by seven men in April of 1972. There are twenty charter members and official incorporation dates from September of 1972. This is an independent church adhering to the Baptist way of governing and having the Holy Bible as sole basis of authority for matters of faith and practise. Its members attempt to live as near as possible in the manner of the first century Christian Church.

At present church members worship in a former commercial structure on Higgins Crowell Road. There is a large Sunday School and a teenage youth group. Three buses provide free transportation.

A weekly radio program, a visitation ministry, and work with shut-ins and prisoners reach out to the community. Other emphases are Child Evangelism, Word of Life Bible Clubs, and support of individual missionaries on the mission field.

Jehovah's Witnesses Kingdom Hall

WALTON STREET, HYANNIS

This Hyannis congregation began in July of 1971, when several families from the Harwich congregation and several from the Falmouth congregation joined together to start work in the central Cape area. Meetings were held in homes at first. Then land was purchased and a Kingdom Hall built on the present site. The building period was from December 1972 to the summer of 1973. Dedication ceremonies were held November 3 and 4, 1973.

The building is a pleasing structure that blends into the surrounding area. The entrance lobby has a cathedral ceiling. A large auditorium, rooms for distribution and storage of magazines and other literature, as well as combination office and library, are included in the facilities.

This congregation is associated with twenty-two others in a circuit in the southeastern Massachusetts area. Assembly activities take place at Natick, where circuits from New England and New York have twice-a-year meetings, usually in spring and winter. There is usually a large national or international meeting each summer.

The Federated Church of Hyannis

MAIN STREET, HYANNIS

This church is a spiritual heir of the old Methodist, Congregational, and Universalist churches and the result of the union of the latter two. Congregational roots go back to the 1830's. When members of two Methodist churches organized the Evangelical Congregational Society, they purchased one of the Methodist buildings. Universalist roots go back to 1829 when fifty people embraced the doctrine of universal salvation. Meeting first in schoolhouses in Hyannis Port and Hyannis, they built their first meetinghouse in 1830 on the site of the above church. Two succeeding buildings built in 1847 and 1873 were each destroyed by fire. In 1904, a Gothic frame structure was erected.

A federation of the two churches was proposed in 1917 and officially incorporated in 1921. The new congregation used the Universalist building for services and the Congregational for recreation. With continued growth more facilities were needed, so Baldwin Hall was built in 1939 and the church acquired Memorial Hall in 1951. Then a new colonial sanctuary was built on the site of the old, with dedication October 19, 1958. A modern parish house addition was constructed on the site of the Memorial building in 1973 to complete an impressive church plant.

Always maintaining a vigorous witness in the community, this church broadcasts its services and holds outdoor summer church at the Hyannis Drive-In. Its organizations, members, and services are characterized by warm friendliness, no doubt due in part to a dedicated ministry spanning several decades.

Greek Orthodox Church of St. George

317 WINTER STREET, HYANNIS

Greek immigrants began arriving on Cape Cod about 1903, settling mostly in Falmouth, Provincetown, and Hyannis. In early years, they traveled to New Bedford on great Holidays for Holy Mass. Occasionally the Greek priest would come to Hyannis to officiate the Divine Liturgy and administer the Sacraments, using the old Odd Fellows Hall. Then in 1939 members bought the present building, the former Grange Hall.

A Greek Language School has been held regularly since 1928, since services are conducted in Greek. In 1939, a Greek Citizens Club and a women's organization were formed. In 1949, the present priest was assigned to the church by the Bishop of Boston. One of 500 in North and South America, the church is headed by an Archbishop in New York City. World Headquarters are in Constantinople, which has been the Holy Seat of Orthodoxy since the fourth century.

The local congregation now has over 250 resident families. Organizations include Greek Orthodox Youth, Choir, Greek Afternoon School, Adult Evening School, Sunday School, and Greek Ladies Philoptochos Society. It is ecumenical. It is headed by a lay president. The sanctuary front has three sections with an altar in the center. It is beautified by candles, portraits of saints and Holy Ikons. A new building is in the planning stages. It will be located at Route 28 and Strawberry Road and will consist of church, classrooms, and administrative center.

Cape Cod Synagogue

145 WINTER STREET, HYANNIS

Members of the Jewish Community met at first in homes for worship. On July 31, 1933, a Jewish Women's Club was organized. The first project was a religious school, which was held in the offices of the late Attorney George Schuman.

A Jewish Men's Club was subsequently formed. This group was responsible for securing a full-time Rabbi and renting space over the present Bradford's Hardware Store.

The present synagogue, of contemporary design, was dedicated July 22-24, 1949. Later the congregation purchased the house on the adjoining property for its religious school.

The Synagogue ministers to the Jewish community of the entire Cape and is a member of the Union of American Hebrew Congregations. A chapter of Hadassah was organized in 1972 in addition to the original women's club. Jewish men are members of B'Nai Brith. The synagogue has always been civic-minded, in addition to assisting with overseas Jewish projects. The first interfaith services on the Cape were held in February 1934 in cooperation with the Federated Church in Hyannis.

Faith Assembly of God

154 BEARSE'S WAY, HYANNIS

A congregation assembled here in 1956 and began worshipping in the basement area of the present church. In 1960, members were joined by the congregation from a small church in South Dennis, which was begun in 1930 by a Salvation Army Worker.

In 1967, the house next to the present church was purchased for a parsonage. Three building programs followed. The modern Sanctuary was built in 1968, with members providing the labor. Other parish facilities were added as funds were available and a youth building is in planning stages.

The church is autonomous, but is affiliated with the Assemblies of God with headquarters in Springfield, Missouri. The local congregation is mission-minded, engaging in a bus ministry and supporting worldwide missions. Church groups include Ambassador's Youth, Royal Rangers, Missionettes, Women's Missionary Council, Kiddie Kollege Nursery School, as well as adult bible study and prayer groups. Teen Challenge, a work with drug addicts, is a project of the Assemblies of God.

First Church of Christ, Scientist

BEARSE'S WAY at STEVENS STREET, HYANNIS

This church, a branch of the Mother Church, the First Church of Christ, Scientist, in Boston, was established in 1943 when the First Church of Christ, Scientist, in Cotuit consolidated with the Christian Science Society in West Yarmouth. The first service of the Hyannis Church occurred on an August Sunday in the Masonic Lodge.

The present site was acquired in 1946. The two buildings formerly used by the Cotuit Church were moved in sections, a distance of about ten miles. The initial Sunday service in this edifice occurred July 3, 1949. The date 1902 is also memorialized on the cornerstone because the first service in the Cotuit Church's original edifice was that year.

As in other branches, each church has its own democratic government. There are no clergy. A First and Second Reader, elected by and from the membership for a limited time, conduct the services. Testimony meetings are held each Wednesday evening. A free public reading room is maintained at 357 Main Street where literature may be read, borrowed, or purchased.

Christian Science was discovered in 1866 and founded by Mary Baker Eddy. It is based on the words and works of Jesus Christ. A distinctive part is its healing of physical disease and sin by spiritual means alone.

First Baptist Church
(AMERICAN BAPTIST)

486 MAIN STREET, HYANNIS

During 1771-1772, sixteen members of the Baptist Church in Harwich who lived in Barnstable obtained consent to form a church in Hyannis. The original meetinghouse had "a great porch all painted red and in which each man bought his ground and built his own square pew."

In 1825, a new meetinghouse was built, having a tower and a bell, for $4,000. About this time members helped build a one-story church in Osterville. Five of the members were licensed to preach in the 1820's and 1830's, and branches of the church were founded in Chatham, Bass River, Falmouth, Mashpee, and Barnstable Village. In 1830, four wardens were chosen to keep good order about the meetinghouse and later another was added to care for the gallery. The church had a circulating library of 350 volumes before the public library began. For music, a bass viol was purchased in 1848 and later a seraphene placed in the gallery. An ell was added to the building in 1866.

The interior of the sanctuary was remodeled and an education wing was begun in 1936, with dedication ceremonies on April 26, 1938. The year 1955 saw further expansion to include a chapel and modern kitchen and dining room. A parsonage, the fourth, was purchased in 1960. In addition to the usual services to parishioners and community, the church was the original home of the Pastoral Counselling Center of the Cape Cod Council of Churches. It also has cooperated in ecumenical ventures with Orthodox, Catholic, and Jewish congregations, and it sponsors a youth center.

St. Francis Xavier Church (Catholic)

347 SOUTH STREET, HYANNIS

This imposing church was dedicated in 1904. The parish was organized earlier, in 1902, meeting in a little church on North Street. Then this larger structure was built on the Hinckley estate on South Street. The house already on the property became the Rectory.

About the year 1916 the church was remodeled. Four beautiful Ionic columns were added to the entrance and the building was lengthened to double the seating capacity. In recent years a Parish Center was built, which houses classrooms, offices, and an auditorium.

This large, active, and ecumenically-oriented parish is known as the church of the President. The Joseph P. Kennedy family worshipped here summers for many years. The sons, who acted as altar boys, later became Senators, Attorney General, and President. John F. Kennedy the Late President, and his family worshipped here before and during his term of office. The second pew in the new chapel bears a plaque marking the seat he habitually occupied. The altar in the main church is a memorial to his eldest brother, Joseph, Jr., who died in war service.

The Saint Francis Christian Missionary Cenacle on South Street houses the Missionary Servants of the Most Blessed Trinity, who coordinate the Religious Education program. Sacred Heart Chapel in Yarmouthport is a mission of St. Francis Xavier Church.

Seventh-Day Adventist Church

HYANNIS

The first Seventh-Day Adventists met in homes and in a hall in East Falmouth. Services were also held at the North Falmouth Congregational Church, the West Falmouth Friends Meetinghouse, and at the Cataumet School House. Their first church, located in Cataumet, was begun in 1950. Meetings were held in the basement area until the church was finished in 1956. Eighty per cent of the work on the church was done by church members.

This church was sold when members decided to be in a more central location. Land was purchased on Route 28 in Osterville. A lovely new structure will be erected soon.

Presently the members hold services on Saturdays in the St. Francis Xavier Parish Hall in Hyannis. These include family Bible classes as well as worship services. This church sponsors clinics to assist people in weight control, eliminating smoking and in health and nutrition. There is a strong missionary emphasis also. The church has all of Cape Cod as well as the islands for its area. There is a small "Company" of Adventists meeting on Martha's Vineyard. It will be called this until it is constituted a church. Headquarters for the church are in Tacoma Park, Washington, D.C.

Church of Christ

336 SEA STREET, HYANNIS

This congregation began in 1962 in Falmouth, when a few people began holding services in the Odd Fellows Building there. Then, seeking a more central location, members purchased the old Captain Angel estate in Hyannis. Plans are now under way for a church to be built on the property.

Each church in this fellowship is independent, though it does have fellowship with others. It endeavors to live first century Christianity in the present day. These churches are worldwide, but the majority of them in this country are in the south. Churches of Christ sponsor Bible colleges and schools for the training of ministers. The governing groups in each congregation are elders and deacons.

Zion Union Church

NORTH STREET, HYANNIS

Because there seemed to be a need for a black-oriented church on Cape Cod, this mission was founded in 1909. A white lay worker from the First Baptist Church in Hyannis and a group of black people together organized the mission and erected the church building.

Services were held mainly during the summer in the early years. The mission served then as the church away from home for many of the Cape's domestic workers who came for the summer. Various visiting clergymen as well as dedicated local laymen and laywomen officiated at the church services and performed pastoral duties through the years.

A permanent pastor was called in June of 1955 and since then services have been held year round. In 1962 the mission was legally constituted as the Zion Union Church. It is an independent interdenominational parish, and the name was chosen to indicate this. A church school was begun in 1965 and an active youth program instituted. Each summer there is an influx of summer people who worship here. Many improvements have been made to the building and currently there is a building program in the planning stages.

Cavalry Baptist Church

WEST MAIN STREET AT LINCOLN ROAD, HYANNIS

In April of 1957, members of a small prayer and Bible study group met to organize a church. The first Sunday service was held in February 1958 at the Masonic Hall. A parcel of land was donated anonymously in June of 1958. Official organization came September 11, 1958, with a charter membership of nine.

A Chapel building from Otis Air Force Base was purchased for $100. It was disassembled and moved to its present site in August of 1959. Work was completed and the first service held on Palm Sunday in April of 1960.

Growth has been steady in fellowship, membership, and service, enabling the parish to buy a parsonage on Arrowhead Drive. Also, the basement area of the church was remodeled into classrooms and the exterior shingled.

Missionary emphasis continues high and support is sent to Africa and Canada as well as to projects in this country. Sunday School and youth work are also major emphases. The inscription on the cornerstone of the church is key to its labors "For the Word of God and the testimony of Jesus Christ."

St. Andrews-By-The-Sea (Episcopal)
IRVING AVENUE, HYANNIS PORT

Episcopal services were first held in Hyannis Port during the summer of 1897 in Union Chapel. Then Episcopalians met successively in Red Men's Hall and the Universalist Church, Hyannis. Captain Hinckley's barge conveyed the congregation to the church.

In 1899 the old red District 5 Schoolhouse was rented. This was no longer used as a school and was furnished as a chapel providing a satisfactory meeting place. It was open on Sundays from the last of June through mid-September. A meeting was held in 1903 to consider buying land for a permanent chapel.

About this time, the Whittemore family offered land at the crest of Sunset Hill, which was gratefully accepted. In August 1906 the cornerstone of the lovely stone chapel was laid with Bishop Whitehead of Pittsburgh presiding. Five years later on August 12, 1911, the church was consecrated by Bishop William Lawrence of Massachusetts.

The Chapel has a commanding view of Nantucket Sound, Squaw Island, and Hyannis Port and is a lovely place to worship on summer Sundays.

Union Chapel
WACHUSETT AVE, HYANNIS PORT

On August 31, 1889, in the parlors of the old Hallet House, the Union Chapel Association was formed. Land was given by the Scudder family for a chapel. John Hinckley and Sons of Yarmouthport erected the first building which was dedicated August 30, 1890. A prestigious list of summer residents were officers and committee members. Emminent guest preachers from many denominations officiated.

Services were held summers only those first few years, but between 1901 and 1915 winter residents arranged for year round services with student ministers from Andover Newton Theological Seminary.

One of those who performed at benefit concerts for the chapel was John Reid, who introduced golf to this country from Scotland. He sang Scottish songs that invariably produced cries for many encores.

During the hurricane of September 1944 the Chapel was demolished. Old timbers were saved, however, and incorporated into the new white frame structure. This was ready for occupancy August 1945. Walter Gaffney Associates were the architects. A sacristy was added in 1962 and a steeple in 1964. On August 23, 1964, a service was held to dedicate the steeple and to commemorate the 75th year of Union Chapel Association. This interdenominational Chapel is open each summer Sunday.

Craigville Tabernacle
(United Church of Christ)

CRAIGVILLE GREEN, CRAIGVILLE

In 1872, when the first camp meeting was held here by the Christian Denomination, a tent church was erected on Christian Hill, the highest piece of land. By 1887, this permanent structure was erected, though sides were left open in keeping with the Biblical term Tabernacle.

The village, named for Dr. J. Austin Craig, an early Christian minister and second President of Antioch College, became the setting each summer for religious and educational conferences. It also became a popular vacation area. The Tabernacle was always the center of activity, along with beautiful Craigville Beach.

In recent years the Tabernacle has been remodeled and redecorated. A new redwood chancel, concrete floor, conference room, and bookstore have been added. In 1960, a Hook and Hastings tracker organ, built the same year as the Tabernacle was given by Wellesley College. Antique benches were still retained, however, and the sides still open to nature on warm summer Sundays.

Though owned by the Christian Camp Meeting Association, the Center is now operated by the Massachusetts Conference United Church of Christ. Services are held here mornings and evenings each Summer Sunday. Conference groups also use it spring and fall, as long as the warm weather lasts.

Our Lady of Victory (Catholic)

SOUTH MAIN STREET, CENTERVILLE

Ground was broken in February of 1957 for this church on six acres of land given by the Herbert Kalmus family. The church was built similar to St. Joseph's Church in Dighton. Bishop James Connolly blessed the church on June 28, 1957. Pews were given by the St. James Church in New Bedford, and the first Mass said July 7, 1957. Built on a pine-surrounded knoll and having a large parking area, it is strategically located in the center of Centerville.

The sanctuary is large and spacious. Decorated in light tones and of simple, classic design, it fits well into the Cape atmosphere. The bells in the steeple were also given by the Kalmus family and regularly ring out the Angelus and hymns.

When the parish was established, it had about 300 people, but now parishioners number over 2,000 souls. A Rectory on Park Avenue was purchased in 1958. Since 1959 the church has been responsible for Our Lady of Hope Chapel and the surrounding area.

A St. Vincent dePaul Society, Men's Club, Women's Guild, C.C.D. Education, and Catholic Youth Organization provide outlets for Christian living and for service in as well as beyond the parish. The active parishioners assist in the emergency FISH organization and other ecumenical activities in cooperation with its village neighbor, South Congregational Church.

South Congregational Church
(United Church of Christ)

MAIN STREET, CENTERVILLE

A branch of the East Parish Church of Barnstable, this church originally was built on the north side of Phinney's Lane in 1796. The minister preached here the fourth Sunday of each month. The other Sundays south side residents had to journey to Barnstable for worship. Their custom was to leave their old shoes by the large rock on Phinney's Lane and put on their Sunday shoes for church, reverting to their old ones on the way home.

In 1816 the South Parish Church was officially organized with nine members. Churchgoers carried footstoves in winter, since there was no heat. Sunday School started in 1822. In 1828 the church was moved to its present site. It was dismantled and carried by ox cart. New articles of faith and covenant were adopted in 1840. A steeple and bell were added to the church in 1848. In this era the organ blower was paid $.10 each service!

In recent years, the belfry clock, made by Turret and Marine Clock Co. of Boston with an 1858 Patent, was electrified with contributions made by villagers. The Christian Education Plant was built in 1955 and a Parish Hall and more classrooms added in 1965.

Parishioners join with those of Our Lady of Victory in an ecumenical witness. Lay groups of all ages and interests evidence community and worldwide concern. Adventures in Reading, Yokefellow Prayer-Study Fellowship, work with patients at Centerville Nursing Home are but a few of their many efforts.

St. Peter's Chapel (Episcopal)

WIANNO AVENUE, WIANNO

In July of 1903, this simple frame chapel was opened for services. The Rector of St. Mary's Episcopal Church in Barnstable was instrumental in organizing the chapel and was preacher the first Sunday. The Chapel was intended for the use of the area's many summer residents and is only kept open in warm months of the year. Vacationing clergymen conduct the services.

The structure is somewhat like that of St. Mary's Church and was designed by Architect Lawrence Hill and built by Chester Bearse. It seats about 115. It is an independent Chapel with support mainly from summer parishioners.

Osterville Baptist Church

824 MAIN STREET, OSTERVILLE

This historic white steepled church in the center of the village was built in 1838 for a few thousand dollars. Its original membership included old Cape names such as Lovells, Halletts, Blounts, Jones, Robbins, Bearses, Hinckleys, Smalls, Allens, and Kelleys.

In the late 1950's several classrooms and the Coleman Auditorium were added. In 1973 eight more classrooms were added, the sanctuary was renovated and the entire plant redecorated and provided with a new heating system.

The church is noted for its musical talent and for involvement in such spiritual activities as Christian Business Men, Gideons, International, and Cape Cod Broadcasting Association. It broadcasts its own evening service. The parish supports twelve missionary families, three of whom are from this church. It is a charter member of the Conservative Baptist movement, is evangelical, and its members represent a wide range of business activities in the community.

Our Lady of Assumption Church (Catholic)

WIANNO AVENUE, OSTERVILLE

The first Catholic services in this village were held in summer during the late 1800's in Veterans Hall with clergy from St. Francis Xavier Parish in Hyannis officiating. The home of Catherine and Charles Daniel, the first resident Catholic family, was the site of catechism classes. By 1904 the mission was established by the Fall River Diocese, as a responsibility of St. Francis Xavier Church. The church construction began that year and was completed and dedicated in 1905.

In 1916 the church was remodeled and rebuilt with double the seating capacity, since the Catholic population was growing. By 1928, the church was established as a separate parish. In 1960 a new front and two wings were added to the church, giving it the shape of a cross. In keeping with the emphasis on renewal, the sanctuary was renovated in 1966.

On the lovely campus type grounds there are also a Rectory and a parish activities house called The Cenacle. Parishioners are active through lay organizations like the Women's Guild, St. Vincent de Paul Society, and the Catholic Youth Organization, with community as well as parish outreach. The Parish is also responsible for two missions--in Santuit and in Mashpee.

United Methodist Church

57 POND STREET, OSTERVILLE

In 1812, a Barnstable Methodist preacher began services in Marstons Mills which resulted in a permanent class in 1819. This new Methodist Episcopal Society received a gift of land from Allen Marstons and moved to it a meetinghouse purchased from the Yarmouth Society.

Osterville members decided in 1846 they had enough strength for their own building and erected one the following year. The two Societies shared ministers for many years. After World War II for thirty-three years the church served as a community church. Then in 1957 it reorganized as a Methodist Church.

A major change occurred in June of 1968 when the Osterville and Marstons Mills parishes merged into one. Just two years later members moved into this beautiful new colonial building. Dedication service for this church plant, which includes offices, sanctuary, and parish house, was June 21, 1970. The spacious parish house includes a parlor, robing room, modern kitchen, classrooms and parish hall decorated in shades of green.

The sanctuary has an impressive cross, which was constructed by parishioners. A parsonage is near by.

The community interest continues as the church opens its doors to many groups. Mission interest too is strong, especially for Vellore Medical Center, where a relative of the Scudder family served for so many years, and for Henderson Settlement in Kentucky.

Cotuit Federated Church

SCHOOL STREET, COTUIT

The inhabitants of old Cotuit (the present Santuit) and Cotuit Port (the present Cotuit) early felt the need for a church. This culminated in 1846 when Methodists belonging to the Marstons Mills Church, as well as some Baptists and Congregationalists, united to form the Union Religious Society of Cotuit.

In one evening many sea captains subscribed $1,000 for the building fund for the "Little White Church on the Hill". This forerunner of the ecumenical spirit was a beacon to mariners coming into port. In 1900, when this society reorganized to a Congregational Church, the Methodists decided to build. In 1901, the church pictured above was built and the Methodist Society formed.

In 1923, Congregationalists and Methodists joined again, using the Methodist property. The old Union Chapel became the home of Mariner's Lodge.

The Federated Church sanctuary was remodeled in the mid-1930's. Bruce Hall, a separate building, was turned and attached to the church about 1959. Classrooms and a modern kitchen were added then. A parsonage is about a block away from the church.

Though the church has remained a Methodist and United Church Federation, it has a community outlook and outreach. "We can agree to disagree but resolve to love and serve." Also, "While we rejoice in the heritage of the years gone past, we look forward to continuing our service and love...in the future".

Saint Jude's Chapel (Catholic)

MAIN STREET (ROUTE 28), SANTUIT

Early in Cape history the Portuguese settled the little community of Santuit, bringing the Catholic faith with them. The first recorded family is that of Jacqueline and Antone Matias, who came from the Azores in 1900 to pick cranberries. In 1902, when the Madeiros family wished their daughter Isobel baptized, she was taken to Oak Bluffs. It was necessary to go by horse and carriage to West Barnstable, by train to Woods Hole, and by boat to Martha's Vineyard.

First services were held once a month in an old schoolhouse or in homes. Later the abandoned schoolhouse on Main Street was renovated and became the first Catholic mission in the Santuit-Cotuit area. Communicants kept the black, pot-bellied stove going and made the benches, kneelers, and a white painted altar. Confessions were heard before the Mass with a screen and kneeler serving as the confessional.

In 1939 the present lovely, classic, colonial chapel was built on land donated by the Frank Frasier family. It was dedicated July 7, 1940, and it is a mission of the Our Lady of the Assumption Parish in Osterville. In recent years, the basement was made into a place for catechetical instruction for the children. Recently also, the altar was changed to face the people in keeping with Church renewal as set forth in Vatican II.

First Pentacostal Church of Christ

ROUTE 130, MASHPEE

Members of the church first met in homes, then in the Mashpee Town Hall. In 1930, the members designed and built their own church on the present site. Parishioners came from various towns in the southwestern section of the Cape.

It is part of the Pentecostal Assembly of the World, which has headquarters in Indianapolis, Indiana. Local emphasis is on youth, with a choir and weeknight meeting held, in addition to regular Sunday Services. Missionary work is another emphasis, with a special offering for missions and a Sunday afternoon missionary meeting held each month.

Mashpee Baptist Church
(AMERICAN BAPTIST)
GREAT NECK ROAD, MASHPEE

Four Wampanoag Inidans, one Narragansett Indian, one black man and one white man were incorporators for the Mashpee Baptist Church in 1898. One Wampanoag, Watson F. Hammond, was a representative to the General Court from Barnstable County, as well as a spiritual leader. His wife was daughter of the famed Indian preacher, Blind Joe Amos, and his son was appointed the church's first secretary.

The Mashpee Wampanoag Praying Indians had embraced the Baptist denomination in the early 1800's. They were influenced by Rev. Joseph Amos who was ordained by the Baptists in 1834. The first meeting place of the church was the Temperance Society Hall. Later the building was called the Chapel. The incorporation meeting of 1898 was held here with seven incorporators named as trustees. Membership at that time was seventy-five.

In 1935, the Chapel burned and the members held services in the Town Hall while the present building was erected. The church presently serves as a community church "standing as a beacon to all people of the town, especially the natives."

The same congregation supports and maintains the historic Old Indian Church and its minister serves both. A Teen Center reaches out to youth. The Men's Fellowship and the Thursday Nighters are also connected with the parish.

Old Indian Church (Baptist)
(AMERICAN BAPTIST)

ROUTE 28, MASHPEE

The oldest church building on Cape Cod is this historic old Indian meetinghouse which was built in 1684 on Briant's Neck in Santuit. Richard Bourne, missionary to the Indians of the upper Cape, held services there under a great oak prior to this time. A special gift of hand-hewn lumber, given by English philanthropists and hauled overland by ox-cart, made the new church possible.

In 1717 the church was moved to its present site and remodeled. It was remodeled again in 1923 and completely restored and rededicated in 1970. An old millstone is by the front door. A simple pulpit, box pews, and a tiny gallery grace the interior, which is kept open for visitors in the summer. The surrounding graveyard with headstones, like Chief Big Elk and Deacon Zacheus Popmonet, are a reminder that this is one of the oldest Indian congregations in America.

Originally Congregational, the parish became Baptist under the leadership of the Indian preacher William Apes. He was a Pequot Indian, later adopted by the Mashpee Tribe and he helped the Indians in regaining lost freedoms. Another Indian preacher with great influence was Blind Joe Amos, who also was a Baptist. In addition to historic occasions, the Indian community holds services on special Sundays in the summer. The officiating minister is the Pastor of the Mashpee Baptist Church.

Queen of all Saints Chapel (Catholic)

GREAT NECK ROAD, MASHPEE

Though Mashpee has a long history as an Indian community, the Roman Catholic history is recent. In 1660 Mashpee was set aside by the Commonwealth of Massachusetts for the Indians of Cape Cod and it has remained so. An influx of white people came with the resort era, but particularly with the development of New Seabury and its thirteen clustered villages. Since there was a fast growing Catholic summer population, masses were held at Popponesset Community Center. These became a mission of Our Lady of Assumption Parish in Osterville in 1960.

In January of 1964, six acres of land on Great Neck Road were deeded to the Fall River Diocese by the Fields Point Corporation, sponsors of New Seabury. The church building was constructed in 1968.

The lovely contemporary structure was planned as a multi-purpose building with portable seating for 700 people. It is the first prefabricated steel building for church use in the Diocese. The great roof spans an unobstructed area 80 by 96 feet. Plans provide for future expansion of the wall at the sanctuary end if necessary. Architect was Robert Sims of Osterville, and it was built by the Karniala Company of West Yarmouth. Distinctive white oak sanctuary furnishings were by craftsmen from the Marney and Lahteine Company of Osterville.

The mission is the responsibility of Our Lady of Assumption Parish. The services at the Popponesset Community Center were discontinued when this new church was built.

Waquoit Congregational Church
(United Church of Christ)

ROUTE 28, WAQUOIT

On March 24, 1847, ten men met and "agreed with each other to associate themselves together in building a meeting house in that part of East Falmouth called "Waquoit." The present strategic site was chosen and plans laid for a building 41 feet long, 31 feet wide, and 16 feet high. The ceiling was to be arched and the outside given two coats of paint. In June 1847, the committee authorized Gilbert Willard of Dartmouth to build this by November 1847 for $1,350.

The treasurer was authorized to sell the pews and give deeds to purchasers in June of the following year. Those pews not sold were rented. Prudential Committee members were chosen from the purchasers, then pews were taxed to pay operating expenses. The legal organization came September 4, 1848, and the official name was Second Congregational Meeting House of East Falmouth.

The first minister was called and a sexton hired in March of 1849. The next April the church assumed care of the burial grounds. At first male members only voted, but by 1858 the word "male" was omitted from the call of the meeting.

The name was changed to Waquoit Congregational Church in March of 1863. Through the years it was not always open full time, though usually it was kept open in summer. With increased population, by 1954 the church took on new vitality and operated year round. A parish house was built in 1960 and a Women's Fellowship was organized. Dedicated clergy and parishioners continue to give this small parish an impact on the community.

Jehovah's Witnesses Kingdom Hall

ROUTE 28, FALMOUTH

The first congregation of Jehovah's Witnesses originated in this area about 1942 when a small group convened. Meetings were held in homes and in a hall in Teaticket.

Land was purchased on Route 28 about 1946. Then a building was moved over the Sagamore Bridge to the site. The structure was formerly the Women's Sewing Club of Plymouth. This was renovated and was used for meetings beginning in 1948.

An addition was made to the building around 1964 and another currently is in progress.

Government of the congregation is by a body of elders. These rotate so that each year one serves as Presiding Overseer.

St. Thomas' Chapel (Catholic)

FALMOUTH HEIGHTS RD., FALMOUTH HEIGHTS

This wood frame building was originally a tea room. In 1928 it was rebuilt for a chapel for summer residents. It is located on Falmouth Harbor and has an expansive view.

This mssion chapel is a responsibility of the St. Patrick's Church in Falmouth, whose priests celebrate the masses each summer.

St. Anthony's Church (Catholic)

ROUTE 28, EAST FALMOUTH

When the Portuguese came to Cape Cod, lured by the high wages of the whaling industry, many settled in East Falmouth. They attended church at St. Joseph's Church in Woods Hole. In 1921, members appealed to the Fall River Diocese for a Portuguese-speaking priest and Rev. Antonia Fortuna was assigned. First services were held in St. Anthony's Hall on Brick Kiln Road later that year and were for all Portuguese-speaking people on Cape Cod.

The 36-acre John Crocker estate was purchased and the homestead, once a sea captain's dwelling, became the Rectory. The present church was built and opened to the public on January 1, 1923. Though the interior was designed colonial, its decor reflected the traditions and customs of the mother country.

When further space was needed, a former dance hall was moved near the church and dedicated January 1934 as a Parish Hall. In 1946 the noted Portuguese artist Henrique Medina painted for the church a magnificent canvas of the apparition of Our Lady of Fatima. This was installed near the altar in 1951 when the church was remodeled. Landscaping was done and a parking area constructed. In a major building program during 1969-70, a new sacristy was added, the basement renovated, and the sanctuary enlarged.

Portuguese-speaking priests are still assigned, though services in that language were discontinued in the 1950's. The church is a reminder, however, of one of the many ethnic groups contributing to Cape Cod life, as well as a lasting tribute to their faith in God.

Falmouth Baptist Church

60 CENTRAL PARK AVENUE, FALMOUTH

The beginnings of this church were in a Bible Study Fellowship originating in 1949 and meeting in the old Falmouth Community Center. A succession of clergymen from Camp Good News, Osterville Baptist Church, and Barrington Bible College provided leadership.

On January 9, 1953, in the Quissett home of the Milton Kelleys, during a prayer meeting, the church was born, officially organizing with fourteen charter members. By 1956 work was begun on a church building on land given by the John Tobeys. Services were held in the basement until 1959 when the auditorium was dedicated. A new parsonage was also built about this time.

By 1963 an overflowing Sunday School and an expanding program caused additional building needs and ground was broken for the present sanctuary. About this time clergy leadership became full time.

The parishioners maintain an active missionary program and a missionary outreach. A Minister to Youth augments the full-time ministry, which reaches out to the community through "Church Time" radio broadcast.

Church groups include Pioneer Girls, College and Career Fellowship and the High School "Believer's Trust Company".

A twentieth anniversary was celebrated in 1973 with appropriate ceremonies.

St. Patrick's Church (Catholic)

MAIN STREET, FALMOUTH

At first this church was a mission of St. Joseph's in Woods Hole. Around the turn of the century, the church was built on Main Street. Then, in 1932, the same year the church was made a full parish, the handsome rectory was built. A statue of St. Patrick has a place of honor in the sanctuary since he is the patron saint of the church.

The interesting exterior is of frame construction, capped with a tower over the main altar. It is a cross-shaped church and has two side altars. There is a Spanish influence in decorations inside. There are also beautiful memorial stained-glass windows in St. Patrick's green.

About 1960 the basement area was enlarged and remodeled to include St. Patrick's Hall and classrooms. The active parish has the usual organizations for all ages, and religious instruction classes for children after school. It makes available its plant to community organizations as part of its outreach.

John Wesley United Methodist Church

270 GIFFORD AVENUE, FALMOUTH

The first records of Methodist interest go back to 1809 when meetings were held in the home of Captain Stephen Swift. Incorporation of the Methodist Society of Falmouth and Sandwich officially came on June 10, 1811. A meetinghouse was erected that year near the cemetery, east of Falmouth village. In 1829, William Nye deeded to the society a half acre of land on Main Street near the central part of town. The church was moved there in 1848. It apparently did not weather the move too well, for the old church was taken down and a new building erected shortly after. Three daughter churches were formed about this time. They were West Falmouth in 1857, East Falmouth in 1859, and Woods Hole in 1884. Only the West Falmouth church now remains and it forms with the Falmouth church the Falmouth United Methodist Parish.

In 1958, a beautiful new contemporary brick church was built on Gifford Street. The name was changed to John Wesley United Methodist at that time. Designed by Hellman and Wilson, the plant includes an education wing, offices, and a sanctuary with bowed arches and a pleasing expanse of glass. The spacious sanctuary has a large window beyond the altar, which brings in the outdoors, and also gives a glimpse of the interior to passers by.

The most unique feature of the church is probably the garden chapel. Its chancel area is filled with plants and there is a small fountain in the center with domed glass overhead.

Saint Barnabas Memorial Church (Episcopal)

MAIN STREET, FALMOUTH

In 1888, through the efforts of the Rev. Phillips Brooks of Boston's Trinity Church, an Episcopal parish was established in Falmouth. The vision and generosity of the Beebe family, Falmouth's first "manoral" summer residents, made possible the beautiful church building. It was designed by Henry Vaughn and dedicated to the memory of the James Madison Beebes. The cornerstone was laid in 1889 and construction proceeded with granite blocks of mountain meadow and sandstone from the same quarry as that which supplied Trinity Church. The Beebe family also gave as a memorial the imposing Saint Barnabas House and built a Carriage Shed.

The beautiful campus-like three-acre setting now includes a Rectory, the former 18th Century Bodfish House and Saint Barnabas Hall which houses offices, classrooms, and an auditorium. The former Carriage Shed has now become a lovely sunlit Chapel, given by the William Peters in memory of their parents. It is connected to the Hall by a cloister overlooking a formal garden and a view of Sider's Pond and Nantucket Sound.

Named for the missionary Barnabas (meaning son of encouragement), the Parish is living up to its name. In addition to encouraging its communicants, it encourages the community at large, opening its doors to the Interfaith Choir, Day Care Center, Scouting programs, clothing depot, and a variety of community interest groups.

The First Congregational Church
(United Church of Christ)

68 MAIN STREET, FALMOUTH

The first village meetinghouse was erected in 1708 near the ancient cemetery off Locust Street on Elm Road. This church burned and a second building was erected on this site. Then a third structure was erected on the Village Green in 1798 using some of the timbers from the previous church.

This edifice had 16 little windows with panes 7" x 9" on each side. Deacon Elijah Swift gave a reed organ. A bell ordered from Paul Revere cost $338.94 and weighed 807 pounds. On it is inscribed "The living to the church I call, and to the grave I summon all." It is said the leader of the church choir tuned his bass viol to the pitch of the bell.

In 1858 the church was moved to its present location just off the Village Green. It was extensively repaired and remodeled at this time and balconies were added. A new education wing was added in 1958. The sanctuary, which seats 450 people, was renovated and restored in 1964. Next to the church stands the very beautiful old federal parsonage, originally the Robinson Bodfish house.

Parishioners are active in community services through their various church organizations and by opening their building to community groups. In the 1960's the parish pioneered in the youth coffee house movement when The Lighthouse was held here in summer months.

Church of the Messiah (Episcopal)

22 CHURCH STREET, WOODS HOLE

Early leaders who organized this oldest Episcopal Church on Cape Cod were Jeremiah Hopkins, local innkeeper and member of the Church of the Messiah in Boston, and Joseph Fay, the first summer resident, who contributed three acres of land near the old burying ground. There were then more than 40 houses in the village and residents had a five-mile carriage ride to Falmouth for church.

The members incorporated in 1852 and built the first sanctuary which was consecrated in 1854. A rectory, contributed by Joseph Fay, was built in 1877. The present magnificent stone church was also a gift of Fay and was erected in 1888, consecrated in 1889. The original church structure is now called the Exchange Building and houses the thrift shop and Omnibus, the alternate High School for the community.

In more recent years, in 1953, a modern rectory was built on the site of the old one. Then, in 1965 the contemporary Fisher House was built across the road. This houses church school classes and a variety of meetings for church and community. The parish continues its long history of outreach in the community and world with a full-time director to help parishioners find and respond to community needs. There is also a House Church (or lay forum) held in connection with the Marine Biological Laboratory.

St. Joseph's Church (Catholic)

MILLFIELD STREET, WOODS HOLE

In 1882, the third Roman Catholic parish on Cape Cod was established at Woods Hole. The boundaries included Woods Hole, Falmouth, Hyannis, Yarmouth, Martha's Vineyard, and Nantucket. The pastor, Rev. Cornelius McSweeney, held services in homes regularly in four areas for twenty years.

"See you in a month," Father McSweeney would call as he set sail for the islands, many times in a gale. His weeping parishioners were sure he would be lost at sea.

The church was responsible for the beginnings of several other parishes through the years but at the present time has as a mission Immaculate Conception Church in North Falmouth.

The frame church has an interior of dark finish that is beautifully decorated, more elaborate than its simple exterior. The Rectory is a large, imposing Victorian structure.

Across the street from the church is an unusual bell tower given by Mrs. George Lillie in 1929. The large bell, named Mendell, reads, "I will teach you of Life and Life eternal." The smaller bell, called Pasteur, reads, "Thanks be to God." The Angelus, the two bells ringing in harmony, rings out three times a day across the harbor.

First Church of Christ, Scientist

CORNER of PALMER and LAKEVIEW AVENUES, FALMOUTH

Though Christian Science meetings were held in homes in the area beginning in 1900, it was not till 1934 that the group was officially designated as a Christian Science Society, a branch of the Mother Church in Boston. The year 1942 saw both the incorporation of the Society and the dedication of its building. The official designation of a church came in September of 1954.

On October 25th, 1942, the dedication service was a particularly joyous occasion since it signified "the externalization of the spiritual thought of church members" and celebration of a building free of debt. The structure is of classical design, simplified to suit a Cape Cod town.

The congregation has a consistent outreach to the community. It maintains a reading room on the Town's Main Street and sponsors free lectures. In addition, it joins other Christian Science churches in sponsoring a Bookmobile in the summer and in holding services in the Barnstable and Plymouth houses of correction. The Literature Committee supplies book boxes containing literature and the Christian Science Monitor in laundromats, bus depots, and other places where people gather. There is also a Sunday School.

Christ Lutheran Church

BRICK KILN ROAD, FALMOUTH

A group of Lutheran families at Otis Air Force Base felt the need of a Lutheran congregation and organized in 1960. The first service was held September 18, 1960, in the building that was then the Seventh-Day Adventist Church in Cataumet. Since then, regular services, Sunday School, and Bible classes have been held. At first, supply ministers were obtained from Lutheran Churches in West Barnstable and Plymouth. In 1961, the church formally affiliated with the Missouri Synod.

In June of 1961 an old Air Force Base Chapel was purchased and in 1962 the present site of ten acres was purchased. Charter membership Sunday was held October 28, 1962, with eighty-four members received. Ground-breaking ceremonies were held December 9 of that year. In February 1963, the first full-time pastor was installed. About this time the church and parsonage were completed, though additional building is still contemplated in the undercroft of the church.

Ecumenical interests have always been a concern of this parish. The Falmouth Interfaith Choir was started here, with the pastor as director and a Catholic priest as organist. Although most families were from the military in early years, now the vast majority are local residents from several Cape Cod towns. Three members of this young parish have now entered full-time church work.

Unitarian Fellowship of Falmouth

ROUTE 28, WEST FALMOUTH

The Unitarian Fellowship of this town was founded in the spring of 1959 by six to eight families of the Unitarian-Universalist persuasion and sponsored by the Unitarian Church of Barnstable. A fellowship is defined as a group of interested persons joining for mutual instruction, worship, and fellowship which may lead to a formal church with building and minister. This was the first such Unitarian-Universalist fellowship in Massachusetts.

First services were held in the Falmouth Community Building and Sunday School was held in various Halls in Woods Hole. Since 1962, however, the fellowship has been able to share the Friends Meetinghouse in West Falmouth. Sunday School classes are combined with those of the Friends. Worship services are held on the first and third Sundays and are conducted by visiting clergy of various denominations as well as by the consulting minister from Barnstable. The year-round membership of about fifty is augmented in warm months by many summer visitors.

United Methodist Church

MAIN ROAD, WEST FALMOUTH

In the year 1850, a Falmouth Methodist minister held a meeting in the village and a number of conversions resulted. A class was formed, and, although some of the young converts were forbidden to attend, they persisted. By 1852 services were being held in the old schoolhouse.

In 1857, a building committee was chosen and Alvin Crowell employed to erect a church. The site was across the street from the present church. Dedication was held later that year, with twenty-two members being dismissed from Falmouth to join the new church.

The present structure was erected in 1900 and dedicated on July 9, 1901. In February 1907 the burning of the mortgage was held with fitting ceremony. About 1936 a minister's study and modern facilities were added. A new organ was dedicated in 1946 and a heating system installed in 1952. Further building and renovations were made in 1957 and completed Easter Sunday 1957.

This church became part of a United Methodist Parish in 1958 and is linked with the John Wesley United Methodist Church in Falmouth. "Two churches--one mission" is the parish theme as it seeks to minister to all. Activities are held jointly with the sister church.

West Falmouth Meeting of Friends

ROUTE 28A, WEST FALMOUTH

Friends have been in this community since its beginnings according to the cemetery plot just off Blacksmith Shop Road. The grave yard is surrounded by an iron railing and has just one stone which reads "Friends Cemetery, 1685-69 Graves." The first meetinghouse of the religious society of Friends was built nearby in 1720.

When the main street of the village was built on a lower level, a second meetinghouse was erected in 1771. The present building, a white frame structure with two separate front doors, was built in 1841. Around it are the slate and granite memorials of a cemetery. Here too, the early graves are not individually marked. Across the road (now Route 28A) is the row of stalls where horses of worshippers were sheltered during services.

This meeting is a preparative meeting, part of the Sandwich Monthly Meeting of Friends. Its Sunday morning worship meetings are silent, or unprogrammed meetings, with members speaking out of the silence on subjects which concern them as they are moved by the Inner Light. Quaker House, which is just behind the meetinghouse, was purchased a few years ago for Sunday School classes, business meetings, and religious gatherings and retreats. West Falmouth Friends join with the wider Quaker Fellowship in furthering peace and education, and in assisting the victims of natural catastrophes or war. The Friends also make their buildings available to the Falmouth Unitarian Fellowship.

Immaculate Conception Church (Catholic)

COUNTY RD., NORTH FALMOUTH

This mission of St. Joseph's Church in Woods Hole, was established in 1915. The building was used as a summer theater prior to this time. As early as 1903, however, priests from Woods Hole would travel to this village to celebrate mass.

This parish also shares St. Joseph's Cemetery with the Woods Hole church. When a cemetery was originally needed, twelve men were sent into the woods back of Gifford Street to clear the land. It remains in use to this day.

Early in the 1960's, the church was kept open year round for masses, though prior to that, it was only open in the summer.

North Falmouth Congregational Church
(United Church of Christ)

MAIN ROAD, NORTH FALMOUTH

In 1832, North Falmouth Congregationalists felt the need of a house of worship in their community and built a meetinghouse. In August of 1833, members officially withdrew from The First Congregational Church of Falmouth, forming the North Falmouth Congregational Society. Predominately a Nye family community, 22 of the original 40 members had the surname Nye. "Every organist for the next 100 years was a Nye either by inheritance or marriage." At one time 85 Nyes lived on the main street of the village.

The church bell once hung in the Universalist Meeting House in Sandwich. When Samuel Nye was soliciting funds for its purchase, one man reponded, "I have not money, but I have a good strong horse and I will get the bell here from Sandwich." With many efforts like this, as well as gifts and legacies, the meetinghouse, as well as the cemetery grounds, have been kept renovated and beautiful. Threatened once by fire and once by lightning, it was redecorated and rededicated in 1893.

Community minded from the beginning, the church was the original home of the village library in 1879. Present day services to the area are wide ranging. The Ship is a Youth Center for the village. The XYZ Club is a community Senior Citizens Group with "Xtra Years of Zest." The Thrift Shop makes used clothing and handcrafts available.

East End Meetinghouse
(UNITED CHURCH OF CHRIST)
SANDWICH ROAD, HATCHVILLE

The East End Meetinghouse was built in 1797 when a group who lived in this area formed into a Society. The members were part of the First Congregational Church in Falmouth. In 1821, the Second Church of Falmouth was officially formed, and the Falmouth members became part of the East End church.

The lovely old colonial style building originally faced in another direction. In 1841, a legacy of $10,000 was left by Shubael Lawrence for the support of preaching "provided that said Society at its own expense, turn the present house of worship gable end to the road, put a handsome steeple to the same, put up a bell of sufficient size, paint and keep the same in good repair and forever keep the house standing at the head of the burying ground where it now stands."

By the following year these conditions were carried out. This necessitated turning the building 90 degrees clockwise. In addition, the porch was removed, galleries taken down, and the pulpit lowered. A parsonage is nearby, down a country lane.

In recent years, the church has been open only in the summer and the Falmouth church is again the main place of membership. The church remains part of the Barnstable Association and is connected with the United Church of Christ.

Cataumet United Methodist Church
1091 COUNTY ROAD, CATAUMET

The history of this building began in 1765 as an Indian Meeting House in Bournedale. Rev. Thomas Tupper was the minister and he was paid by the General Court. The Indians did not adopt the white man's religion, however, and the church fell into disuse. In 1799, it was dismantled and moved to South Pocasset (Cataumet) and rebuilt in the cemetery grounds.

Meanwhile, Rev. Joseph Snelling, one of the early itinerants who "faithfully and successfully sowed Methodist seed among the sand dunes of Cape Cod," settled down in Pocasset from 1808 to 1813. He recorded a "large and steady congregation."

In 1839, the church was turned around and a new front with tower and belfry added. Old-fashioned box pews were replaced with "those of modern style." A parsonage was moved from Barlows Landing near the church in 1854. Then in 1893-94 the church was moved across the street. It was raised and a vestry, parlor, and kitchen added. There were also new stained-glass windows and seats for the sanctuary. Shingling and painting completed the renovation. The first service in the present site was May 17, 1894.

A major renovation beautified the church in 1927 when summer people began to affiliate as members. Again in 1963 renovations occurred with addition of classrooms, modern kitchen, and handy dining hall. This active church is part of the Bourne-Cataumet United Methodist Parish.

Cataumet Christadelphian Ecclesia

930 COUNTY ROAD, CATAUMET

This movement began in the area in 1908, when teachers came from Brockton and held services and Bible classes in homes. About this time, Seabury Gibbs moved here from Brockton and services were held in his home. From 1939 to 1948, meetings were moved to the old Cataumet Schoolhouse.

In 1948, Gibbs gave land for a chapel and a basement area was constructed. The members met there until the top section was added in 1951. In 1966, additional facilities including Sunday School rooms were added. There were many artisans among the members, so the building was completely erected by them.

Christadelphia means "brethren of Christ" and members seek a rebirth of first century Christianity. The movement originated in 1948 and is presently strongest in England, Australia, and Canada. The work "ecclesia" is used to avoid the designation of the church as a building rather than a congregation. There are no paid clergymen.

Church of Jesus Christ of Latter Day Saints

COUNTY ROAD, CATAUMET

This church, also called Mormon, began with military personnel at Otis Air Force Base and first meetings were held in a Base Chapel around the year 1960. Soon land was bought at Monument Beach and a small cottage on the property was used as a chapel. It was decided to locate elsewhere and the land was sold. Members then met in a hall in Monument Beach and later in the American Legion Hall in Bourne.

The present chapel was begun in 1966. It was designed by authorities at the church's headquarters in Salt Lake City, Utah, though they consulted with local church members. The contemporary building has a sanctuary, offices, classrooms, baptistry, large meeting room and well-equipped kitchen.

The local growing congregation emphasizes mission work of its members and each young person gives two years' service. There are presently four missionaries on the Cape. Groups within the church include the Mutual Improvement Society for youth and the Relief Society, a ladies' organization. On Sundays all ages attend the Sunday School. Also Priesthood and Sacrament services are held.

An independent Sunday School meets in Dennisport, but is associated with this congregation. The parish encompasses Nantucket, Martha's Vineyard, Cape Cod and beyond to the Plymouth-Kingston line. It is one of fourteen units comprising the Boston Stake, with Headquarters in Weston.

First Baptist Church
(AMERICAN BAPTIST)

300 BARLOWS LANDING ROAD, POCASSET

The much traveled sanctuary of this church began life in the Sandwich-Mashpee area, probably as an old schoolhouse. In 1838, it was moved in sections to the high part of the Pocasset Cemetery, when twelve residents organized the Baptist Church of Christ. At the incorporation meeting, members adopted the principles and practice of the Second Baptist Church of Boston.

By 1890, the center of population had shifted and the church was moved to a plot near the railroad, a process that took two weeks. This was not a unanimous decision, and some unhappy parishioners worshipped for a time in a little interdenominational chapel. This later closed, and is now the Water District office. The Baptist church was redecorated after the move, and Gothic style stained-glass windows installed. In June of 1895, money was collected for a bell, which used to toll the age of deceased members.

The church took its present name in 1954 and the covenant was revised. The sanctuary was filled to overflowing on Sundays, so the Whitmore farm was purchased in 1956. The original parsonage was sold and the Whitmore house used for that purpose. Then, in 1958, the church was moved for the third time to its present location--with not a crack in the plaster. The sanctuary was enlarged to seat 180 and a full basement, baptistry, nursery, and parking area added. A parish house wing was built in 1960. The original church had grown into an impressive physical plant, a worthy base for a vigorous witness in the parish and to the community and world.

St. John the Evangelist (Catholic)

VIRGINIA ROAD, POCASSET

Union Chapel was the scene of the first mass celebrated in Pocasset on Sunday, July 7, 1912. After this, services were held regularly summers in a barn in the rear of Pocasset House on Main Road. Priests from Sandwich were the celebrants. About 1915, services were moved to the carriage room in the new barn owned by George Johnson.

In 1923, a lot was purchased at the intersection of two main streets. A Knights of Columbus Recreation Hut at the Naval Air Station in Chatham was given to the parish. It was moved to the new site and equipped with pews and an altar. The first mass was held on August 24, 1924.

The present lovely English Tudor structure was built in 1931. The interior was oak-paneled. Two beautiful figures of the Virgin Mary and of the Christ were carved in Europe and are part of an arch on either side of the sanctuary. The bell, given in recent years, was cast in Heidelberg, Germany, and is in honor of St. Barbara, patron saint of architects.

A church addition is now being planned. The new Parish Center will soon supplement the sanctuary and rectory, increasing the church plant to more effectively continue its outreach.

The church has only recently attained parish status.

Bourne United Methodist Church

37 SANDWICH ROAD, BOURNE

In 1789, Bishop Asbury appointed Jesse Lee to a circuit of New England where there were no Methodists. He started a class of 13 members in 1791 in Monument (now Bourne)

The first Methodist Episcopal Church was built here in 1831. Captain Ellis M. Swift started the enterprise. He bought the lumber in Maine, shipping it down on his vessel. He hired the carpenters and paid the bills, getting his money back when the pews were sold.

In 1842, the Meetinghouse was enlarged and raised. A vestry was built below it in 1889. A bell, still in use, was given in 1884 by Jonathan Bourne, for whom the town was named. The large reed organ was purchased for the church by the townspeople. This was later moved to the commodious summer chapel built at Monument Beach in 1891. A new organ costing $1,800 was then purchased for the Bourne church.

In 1964, a new addition was built containing classrooms, modern kitchen, and large Crain Hall named for a former pastor. Later the name was changed to Bourne United Methodist Church.

Today the parish is large and active and is associated with the Cataumet United Methodist Church in the Bourne-Cataumet United Methodist Parish. One is reminded of its history, when reflecting that the first Methodist parish has a church which stands on the original site, and contains part of the original Meetinghouse.

St. Margaret's Church (Catholic)

141 MAIN STREET, BUZZARDS BAY

Masses were first held in this town in July 1911 by Rev. John McKeon from Corpus Christi Church in Sandwich. Franklin, Bourne, and Fireman's Halls were used in turn. Also, masses were said in a private home in Bournedale in 1912 for the convenience of the workers on the Cape Cod Canal.

Spurred on by a contribution of $5,000 from summer resident Margaret Hall, the present church was begun. Thomas Helleher of Sandwich was builder. Architects were Maginnis and Walsh of Boston. Mrs. Hall died before the building was completed. In recognition of her gift, the church was placed under the special protection of St. Margaret. Dedication services were held July 4, 1915.

The edifice is of Spanish mission style of architecture, reduced to simple terms in keeping with the surroundings. The altar is of Italian Byzantine style. A Rectory and Parish Center provide additional physical facilities for the thriving parish and its ongoing work. The church has as a mission St. Mary's Star of the Sea Church, Onset.

St. Peter's Church on the Canal (Episcopal)

MAIN STREET, BUZZARDS BAY

Episcopal services in this community began on March 27, 1938, in Red Men's Hall with lay readers and archdeacons serving as leaders. With the coming of Rev. John Stephenson in 1944, activity increased and a building fund started. Contributions came from all over the country when the story of the church, its Teen Town and Father Steve were broadcast on the old Vox Pop radio program.

In early 1947, an unused church in the Town of Hull was secured and floated on a barge across Cape Cod Bay and down the Canal. Then it was moved onto a foundation on its present site. Unused forty years, it needed extensive repair and renovation. A Parish Hall was added in 1948.

In 1963, the church was formally consecrated a parish in the Episcopal Diocese of Massachusetts. A steeple and chimes were added in 1964 and two years later the adjacent property was bought and landscaped. About this time the Church Exchange was founded. The church is currently expanding its facilities again, by converting a building from Otis Air Force Base into extra Parish House facilities for the active congregation.

The interior decoration of the sanctuary has a sea theme. Carved shells and fish adorn the chancel area and pew ends have either a ship or an anchor design. Over the front door is the prow of a ship and a cross symbolic of St. Peter the fisherman for whom the church is named.

Grace Alliance Church
(Christian & Missionary Alliance)

CYPRESS STREET, BUZZARDS BAY

The beginnings of this church were in 1957 when a group of Baptists organized the Community Baptist Church of Bourne. On March 19, 1958, this church became part of the Christian & Missionary Alliance. Meetings were held in a hall on Head of the Bay Road.

On July 20, 1958, a pastor was called and that August services were moved to the Bourne Town Hall. The same summer a fund drive for a new building was launched.

The new church building, of contemporary style, is located near the Bourne Rotary. It was dedicated November 20, 1960. Recently a two year program of redecorating in the classrooms and sanctuary was completed. The latter has a knotty pine ceiling, carpeted center pulpit area with altar rail and pleasing pale blue tint on the white walls.

Organizations include the Women's Missionary Prayer Fellowship, Alliance Men's Fellowship, Pairs and Spares (for young adults) and a film ministry to youth. This active church is part of the New England District and headquarters for the denomination are in New York City.

First Church of Christ, Scientist

36 WASHINGTON AVENUE, BUZZARDS BAY

In 1908 a group of Christian Scientists and their fellow students began meetings in Franklin Hall on Cohasset Avenue, Buzzards Bay. The following year they organized as a Christian Science Society.

In 1910, a lot was purchased on Washington Avenue and the present building was started in 1919. The edifice was completed and paid for in 1921 with the assistance of the Mother Church in Boston. In the meantime, the Society had sponsored its first Christian Science Lecture in 1916.

By 1938 a new wing was added for the Sunday School. In November of that same year the organization became the First Church of Christ, Scientist of Bourne in Buzzards Bay. The church building was dedicated in April of 1942. In 1952 the present name was adoped.

Church members maintain a Reading Room in Buzzards Bay.

Otis Air Force Base Chapels

OTIS AIR FORCE BASE

For many years there have been several chapels at Otis Air Force Base, which is in the Bourne-Sandwich area. In the past, full time Protestant, Catholic and Jewish Chaplains have been stationed there. In those days there were active youth and adult groups in addition to regular services.

In 1973 much of the acitivity at the base was phased out. No full time chaplains have been assigned there since January of 1974. The chapels can be used by National Guard or other military and civilian groups as requested. Upper Cape people occasionally use the chapels for Days of Recollection, Religious Education meetings or other religious events.

Addendum
CHURCHES OF CAPE COD
1974

AMERICAN BAPTIST
    Brewster -- Brewster Baptist Church
    Hyannis -- The First Baptist Church
    Mashpee --Old Indian Church
    Mashpee -- Mashpee Baptist Church
    Pocasset -- First Baptist Church
    Yarmouth, South -- Bass River Community Baptist Church

ASSEMBLY OF GOD
    Eastham -- Grace Chapel, Assembly of God
    Hyannis -- Faith Assembly of God Church

BAHA'I
    Falmouth -- Baha'i Study
    Hyannis -- Baha'i Study

BAPTIST
    Eastham, North -- Nauset Baptist Church
    Falmouth -- Falmouth Baptist Church
    Forestdale -- Forestdale Baptist Church
    Harwich, West -- The First Baptist Church of West Harwich and Dennisport
    Hyannis -- Calvary Baptist Church
    Osterville -- Osterville Baptist Church
    Yarmouth, South -- Evangelical Baptist Church
    Yarmouth, West -- New Testament Baptist Church

CATHOLIC (ROMAN)
    Barnstable, West -- Chapel of Our Lady of Hope
    Brewster, East -- Immaculate Conception Catholic Church
    Brewster, West -- Our Lady of the Cape
    Buzzards Bay -- St. Margaret's Church
    Centerville -- Our Lady of Victory
    Chatham -- Holy Redeemer Church
    Chatham, South -- Our Lady of Grace Church
    Dennisport -- Our Lady of Annunciation Church
    Eastham -- Church of the Visitation
    Falmouth -- St. Patrick's Catholic Church
    Falmouth, East -- St. Thomas' Catholic Chapel
    Falmouth Heights -- St. Thomas' Catholic Chapel
    Falmouth, North -- Immaculate Conception Chapel
    Harwich, West -- Holy Trinity Catholic Church
    Hyannis -- St. Francis Xavier Catholic Church
    Mashpee -- Queen of All Saints Chapel
    Orleans -- St. Joan of Arc Church
    Osterville -- Our Lady of the Assumption Catholic Church
    Pocasset -- St. John's Catholic Church
    Provincetown -- Church of St. Peter the Apostle
    Sagamore -- St. Theresa's Church
    Sandwich -- Corpus Christi Catholic Church
    Santuit -- St. Jude's Chapel
    Truro -- Sacred Heart Church
    Truro, North -- Our Lady of Perpetual Help Church

Wellfleet -- Our Lady of Lourdes Catholic Church
Woods Hole -- St. Joseph's Catholic Church
Yarmouth, Bass River -- Our Lady of the Highway Church
Yarmouth, South -- St. Pius the Tenth Catholic Church
Yarmouthport -- Sacred Heart Church

CHRISTADELPHIAN
Cataumet -- Cataumet Christadelphian Ecclesia
Chatham -- Chatham Christadelphian Ecclesia

CHRISTIAN SCIENCE
Brewster -- First Church of Christ, Scientist, Brewster and Orleans
Buzzards Bay -- First Church of Christ, Scientist
Chatham -- First Church of Christ, Scientist
Falmouth -- First Church of Christ, Scientist
Harwich Port -- First Church of Christ, Scientist
Hyannis -- First Church of Christ, Scientist

CHURCH OF CHRIST
Hyannis -- Church of Christ

CHURCH OF THE CHRISTIAN AND MISSIONARY ALLIANCE
Buzzards Bay -- Grace Alliance Church

CHURCH OF JESUS CHRIST
Cataumet -- Church of Jesus Christ of Latter Day Saints, Cape Cod Branch

CHURCH OF THE NAZARENE
Dennisport -- Church of the Nazarene

CHURCH OF THE NEW JERUSALEM (Swedenborgian)
Yarmouthport -- Church of the New Jerusalem

COMMUNITY CHURCH
Chatham, South -- South Chatham Community Church
Dennis, East -- East Dennis Community Church

COMMUNITY OF JESUS
Orleans -- The Community of Jesus

CONGREGATIONAL
Yarmouthport -- The First Congregational Church of Yarmouth

EPISCOPAL
Barnstable -- St. Mary's Church, Episcopal
Buzzards Bay -- St. Peter's-on-the-Canal
Chatham -- St. Christopher's Church
Falmouth -- St. Barnabas Memorial Church
Harwich Port -- Christ Episcopal Church
Hyannis Port -- St. Andrews by-the-Sea
Orleans -- The Church of the Holy Spirit
Provincetown -- The Church of St. Mary of the Harbor
Sandwich -- St. John's Episcopal Church
Wellfleet -- The Chapel of St. James the Fisherman
Wianno -- St. Peter's Episcopal Chapel
Woods Hole -- Church of the Messiah
Yarmouth, South -- St. David's Episcopal Church

FEDERATED
Cotuit -- The Cotuit Federated Church (Federated, United Church of Christ, and United Methodist)
Hyannis -- Federated Church of Hyannis

FRIENDS
Falmouth, West -- Friends Preparative Meeting
Sandwich -- Sandwich Friends Meeting
Yarmouth, South -- South Yarmouth Friends Meeting

GREEK ORTHODOX
    Hyannis -- Greek Orthodox Church of St. George
JEHOVAH'S WITNESSES
    Falmouth, East -- Kingdom Hall of Jehovah's Witnesses
    Harwich, East -- Kingdom Hall of Jehovah's Witnesses
    Hyannis -- Kingdom Hall of Jehovah's Witnesses
JEWISH
    Hyannis -- Cape Cod Synagogue
LUTHERAN
    Barnstable, West -- First Lutheran Church
    Brewster -- Trinity Evangelical Lutheran Church
    Falmouth -- Christ Lutheran Church of Falmouth
PENTECOSTAL
    Dennisport -- Cape Cod Pentecostal Assembly
    Mashpee -- First Pentecostal Church of Jesus Christ
PRESBYTERIAN
    Barnstable -- Now Forming
REORGANIZED CHURCH OF JESUS CHRIST
    Dennisport - Reorganized Church of Jesus Christ of Latter Day Saints
SEVENTH DAY ADVENTIST
    Hyannis -- Cape Cod Seventh-Day Adventist Church
UNION
    Hyannis -- Zion Union Church
    Hyannis Port -- Union Chapel (Interdenominational)
    Truro, North -- Christian Union Church
UNITARIAN-UNIVERSALIST
    Barnstable -- The Unitarian Church
    Brewster-Eastham First Unitarian-Universalist Parish of Cape Cod:
    Brewster -- First Unitarian-Universalist Church
    Eastham -- First Unitarian-Universalist Church
                                  (Chapel in the Pines)
    Falmouth, West -- Falmouth Unitarian Fellowship
    Provincetown -- The First Universalist-Unitarian Parish of Provincetown
    (SEE ALSO: Sandwich -- First Church of Christ in Sandwich)
UNITED CHURCH OF CHRIST
    Barnstable, West -- West Parish Congregational Church
    Centerville -- South Congregational Church
    Chatham -- The First Congregational Church of Chatham
    Craigville -- Craigville Conference Center (Tabernacle)
    Dennis -- Dennis Union Church
    Dennis, South -- Congregational Church of South Dennis
    Dennis, West -- West Dennis Community Church
    Falmouth -- The First Congregational Church
    Falmouth, North -- North Falmouth Congregational Church
    Harwich -- First Congregational Church
    Harwich Port -- Pilgrim Congregational Church, U.C.C.
    Hatchville -- East End Meetinghouse
    Orleans, East -- Federated Church of Orleans
    Sandwich -- First Church of Christ in Sandwich
    Truro -- First Congregational Church
    Waquoit -- Waquoit Congregational Church
    Wellfleet -- First Congregational Church
    Yarmouth, West -- West Yarmouth Congregational Church

(SEE ALSO: Cotuit -- Cotuit Federated Church)
UNITED METHODIST
- Bourne -- Bourne United Methodist Church
- Cataumet -- Cataumet United Methodist Church
- Chatham-Harwich United Methodist Parish:
- Chatham -- First United Methodist Church
- Harwich, East -- United Methodist Church
- Harwich, South -- United Methodist Church
- Eastham -- United Methodist Church
- Falmouth United Methodist Parish:
- Falmouth -- John Wesley United Methodist Church
- Falmouth, West -- United Methodist Church
- Orleans -- United Methodist Church
- Osterville -- United Methodist Church
- Provincetown -- United Methodist Church
- Sagamore -- Swift Memorial United Methodist Church
- Wellfleet -- Wellfleet United Methodist Church
- Yarmouth, South -- United Methodist Church
- (SEE ALSO: Cotuit -- Cotuit Federated Church)

UNITY
- Unity Study Groups

OTHER CHURCH RELATED GROUPS
- Briarwood Conference Center (Episcopal), Monument Beach
- Craigville Conference Center (United Church of Christ), Craigville
- Cape Cod Council of Churches, Offices- Hyannis
   ---Service Center Clothing Depot, Barnstable
- Fisherman's Players (United Methodist' Church) North Eastham